CONJUGAL TERRORISM: A PSYCHOLOGICAL AND COMMUNITY TREATMENT MODEL OF WIFE ABUSE

By Steven M. Morgan

PALO ALTO, CALIFORNIA

Published By

R & E Research Associates, Inc.

936 Industrial Avenue
Palo Alto, California 94303

PUBLISHERS

Library of Congress Card Catalog Number

V HV   81-83615
6626
.M6   I.S.B.N.
1982
             0-88247-623-8

FOREWORD

Most of us today are all too familiar with terrorism. Terrorists plant bombs, blow up buildings, highjack planes, take people hostage, harm them physically and emotionally and in other ways bully the Establishment for political ends.

Steven Morgan has coined the phrase "conjugal terrorism" to jar us into the realization that wife abuse is, indeed, a form of political terrorism. Battering men wield guns or knives or fists to terrorize "their" women. Many literally hold their wives or lovers hostage -- controlling their every move, isolating them, raping them and holding them captive in the home -- by the use or threat of violence. Battered women are political prisoners. Male domination and protection of the patriarchal system are the political issues at stake.

Those of us who have been working in the field of "domestic violence" are becoming more aware of semantics, of the significance of the words we use and the messages they impart. Domestic violence, marital violence or family violence have become euphemisms for violence against wives. At first these terms were used to draw public attention because there was so much resistance to taking seriously the phenomenon of wife abuse per se. The use of such phrases as domestic or family disturbances, spats, disputes or quarrels are also misleading. They serve to deny the specificity of wife battering, trivialize violence against women in the home, diminish the impact of the violence and prevent people from understanding its reality.

Another example of word usage is the American

III

reference to shelters for battered women and their children. In by book <u>Battered Wives</u> I called them refuges, the term applied in Europe and other foreign countries. It more accurately portrays the women who used these residential facilities as **refugees** - refugees from "conjugal terrorism." While shelters are defined as places of safety, the term does not have the same political connotation. The American public more readily responds to the concept of refugees who flee for their lives. In truth, battered women and their children are refugees who have fled from disastrous conditions, are homeless and in need of emergency services.

Steven Morgan reviews historical, cultural, psychological and political influences on battered women and how they become trapped in violent relationships through learned helplessness and neurotic acceptance. He also reviews the available data on battering husbands and various theories of human aggression and violence. But he adds another dimension that is often overlooked by behavioral scientists: psychopolitics, or the interplay of psychological motives and political decisions. Morgan makes the connection between the need of the husband to maintain power and control over his wife and the use of indiscriminate violence -- the connection between neurotic male pride and conjugal terrorism.

As a prevention strategy, Morgan suggests a community psychology approach to change local conditions in order to improve positive development of persons and reduce reactions to stress. The community systems approach would involve and integrate all of the various grass roots groups and public agencies in providing emergency services and developing long-range prevention programs. These include refuges for battered women and their children, the media, law enforcement, government social service and welfare agencies, mental health, legal aid, hospitals and clinics, alcohol and drug abuse programs, public schools, etc.

Morgan is particularly concerned with counseling of young couples about the hazards they face. They should be made aware of identifying characteristics of abused women and violent husbands and taught how to resolve conflicts without resorting to violence and where to find help if they need it. It is my own belief that non-sexist education needs to begin at the

IV

earliest stages of childhood -- in pre-school nurseries and child care centers. The seeds of dominant-passive male and female behavior patterns are sown long before the primary grades. We need classes in parenting and violence prevention. We need early detection of violence-producing behavior so that we can intervene before it becomes an established pattern.

In the final analysis, as Morgan points out, the community holds the key to the psychological and financial resources that affect wife battering as a phenomenon. The community can keep the problem locked behind closed doors, as it has in the past. Or the community can use the key to open those doors and release these women from their torment. Conjugal terrorism is a social problem, the solution to which requires community support and action. Steven Morgan provides us with many of the tools and strategies necessary in our, hopefully, mutual mission towards a better quality of human life and an end to the Battle of the Sexes.

Del Martin

Author of _Battered Wives_ and Commissioner, California
    State Commission on Crime Control and Violence
                    Prevention

TABLE OF CONTENTS

LIST OF FIGURES

FIGURES

ACKNOWLEDGEMENTS

It is a great honor for me to be able to thank those who have been loving and kind to me while I sought to achieve my goals. To my parents, Bernard and Sophie Morgan, thank you for your unending faith and confidence in me. To Judy and Bob, thank you for your concern and support. To my special friends Bill and Errol, my deepest respect and appreciation for your loving skills. To Doug and Chloe, thank you for your deep and abiding friendship. To Richie and Cathy, thank you for your aid and comfort.

In addition to family and friends, I wish to publicly acknowledge my appreciation to my committee. To Dr. Lelia Veaco, my warmest regards for your generosity and kindness. To Tom Brigham, thank you for your friendship as well as your contributions. To Dr. Bruce Fisher, thank you for your help. To Dr. Alice Sheppard, Special Consultant, a very sincerely felt thank you for your time and energy. Your enormous talent and sense of humor were vital to the completion of this work.

Finally, a note of appreciation for the love and support of Cecile Currier, without whose help this work would not have been possible.

I agree that one may end up in a personality category as the end result of abuse, but we don't start out that way. Does one get out of a marriage when her face is slapped once? I would now, but after being married for two days, I figured I had some adjusting to do.

Within the first six months of my marriage, I tried to discuss marriage counseling with my husband. I offered him an ultimatum: Either we get some help, or I would get a divorce. That was when he threw me on the floor, sat on top of me and poked me repeatedly in the face with his finger. After that, he raped me. I wanted to run out into the street screaming, but I heard myself saying, "Help, my husband raped me." Does our society and our law enforcement and legal system accept rape by a marriage partner as a crime? In a recent survey done by the criminal justice system in the United States, wife-beating was referred to as a "domestic spat".

I was told I would be murdered and was shown how he would do it if I left him. I had no money to retain a lawyer and no family or friends to offer me shelter. I also had no money on which to establish myself.

An Anonymous Letter to
Human Behavior Magazine
(September, 1977)

CHAPTER 1

INTRODUCTION

Wife abuse can be understood as a form of terrorism. The violent husband, viewed as a conjugal terrorist, uses violence to threaten and harass his wife into submission in a manner analogous to the way a terrorist threats his kidnap victim. In both roles the person feels morally superior to the law and paradoxically is respected for what he does. However, the major difference between the two is in the public's reaction toward their respective victims. The hostage in the political kidnapping usually receives empathy and support from public opinion, while the battered wife is ignored and left to fend for herself.

The problem of wife abuse, although centuries old, has only recently gained the attention of mental health professionals. Mental health workers are just becoming aware of how far reaching and potentially destructive its effects are. Violence in the home has contributed to the rise of violence in the general community and has resulted in individual isolation and apathy. It is intimately connected with child abuse and has worked to undermine the stability of the American family. Yet, until 1974, there were no programs for battered wives in the United States.

Until recently help for the battered wife consisted of individual psychotherapy offered at the local mental health clinic. However, there were several problems with that approach. To begin with, when the battered wife came in for help she was usually too ashamed to admit she was beaten by her husband. As a consequence she received help for problems other than

1

the abuse. When she did identify herself as an abused wife, she was often made to feel responsible for the abuse. Another problem was that it was next to impossible to get the husband into treatment with her. Finally, when confronted with the needs of the battered women, the mental health professional did not know how to respond. There were no programs developed and little, if any, published information available.

The purpose of this study is to investigate the elements of wife abuse, to review the literature and to propose models for two community psychology based programs that assist battered women. These programs offer prevention at three strategy levels.

It is assumed that the development of specific programs will eliminate or sharply curtail the problems of treatment. Having programs designed expressly for battered women will encourage the women to identify themselves so that they may be served. These programs should draw concerned staff members who are interested in working with abused women. The programs will additionally act as research tools, generating important first hand information about the women and their husbands that could be disseminated to professionals and lay people working with abused women. The programs will provide vital resources, enabling the women to make choices and exercise options about their futures. Increased options will give the women increased opportunities when deciding whether or not they wish to return to their husbands.

Extent of the Problem

While there is no universally accepted definition of what constitutes a battered wife, Gayford (1977a) offers a useful one in his statement, "a battered wife is any woman who has received deliberate, severe and repeated demonstrable physical injuries from her partner" (p. 283). The significanct elements of the definition are "deliberate, repeated injuries." An occasional slap in the passion of the moment, no matter how degrading and emotionally retarding it may be, does not constitute "beating." The presence of physical damage is important because it satisfies the definition used by the police and courts.

From a psychologist's point of view, there are certain limitations with the definition. Most important is its failure to acknowledge the

2

psychological damage done by the violence.

The full extent of wife abuse is not know. However, Straus (1976) estimates that there are at least 1.5 million battered women throughout the country, and probably twice that number. In a study of women seeking divorce, 20% of the middle-class women and 40% of the working-class women reported that physical abuse was a major problem in their marriages (Levinger, 1966). If one considers that there are 47 million married women in the United States, of whom one third become divorced and one third of these are physically abused, it is estimated that 4.½ million are beaten in this country.

Warrior (1975) reported that "at Boston City Hospital, approximately 70% of the assault victims received at emergency are women who have been attacked in the home" (p. 3). Flynn (1977) reported that 10% of the families he investigated in a northern Michigan county experienced some form of conjugal violence.

In his book titled, The Violent Home, Gelles (1974) examined the extent of violence among 80 families. Based on police reports, half the sample were designated violent, the remainder "not-violent." In the "not-violent" group, 47% of the husbands admitted they hit their wives six or more times a year. Some in the "not-violent" group hit their wives as frequently as every day. The group identified as "violent" reported hitting their wives at least once a year in 75% of the cases, and regularly in 50% of the cases.

Unfortunately, violence escalates unless stopped. Martin (1976) reports from F.B.I. statistics that;

> In 1974, 25 percent of all murders in San Francisco involved legally married or cohabiting mates. Almost 1/3 of all female homicide victims in California in 1971 were murdered by their husbands. Nationwide in 1973 . . . ¼ of all the murders occurred within the family, and ½ of these were husband-wife killings. (p. 45)

Moreover in a survey of homicide cases in Detroit for a 42-year period, 30% of the pairs of victims and assailants were found to be related (Lystad, 1975). A 1965 study for Chicago revealed that almost half the victims were related to the offenders.

Wife abuse ; does not stop with the wife, but

3

affects other family members. As concluded from a study of 100 battered wives in England;

> There appears to be an association between child abuse and wife abuse, with 37 of the women admitting they were discharging frustration on their offspring, and 54 claiming that their husbands had extended their violence to the children. (Gayford, 1975, p. 196)

As The battered woman can be found in every ethnic, religious, and socioeconomic class, the extent of the problem can be best understood in the context of its historical roots. The remainder of this chapter will explore the historical roots of wife abuse.

The History of Wife Abuse

Wife abuse in America has existed since the founding of the Colonies. English Common Law and Christianity, foundations of this nation's culture, accepted wife abuse as the husband's prerogative. "Marital violence was his privilege. In order to find a time in history when wife beating did not enjoy having custom and law on their sided, it is necessary to go back . . . to pre-biblical times" (Davidson, 1977, p. 4).

Jacobsen (1946), writing about Mesopotamian civilization, gave an account of the mythological birth of Gods in the Mesopotamian Cosmos. Through deceit and rope the Mood-God Sin and his brother were born. Jacobsen wrote of their mother, Ninlil;

> This story comes from a society in which woman's honor was an unknown concept. Violation of an unmarried woman was an offense against her guardian; violation of a married woman was an offense against society and its laws. In no case, however, were they offenses against the woman. She and her feelings simply did not count. (p. 155)

Old Testament authors codified the woman's position within the Biblical Hebrew culture. God blamed woman for the fall of man from his grace saying, "I will greatly multiply they sorrow and thy

4

conception: in sorrow thou shalt bring forth children: and thy desire shall be to thy husband, and he shall rule over thee: (Genesis 3:16).

Biblical authors did not consider the male as responsible for his behavior, but chose to see woman as the source of his downfall. "Because thou has harkened onto the voice of they wife, and hast eaten of the tree, of which I commanded thee, saying, Thou shall not eat of it: cursed is the ground for they sake" (Genesis 3:17).

Male distrust of the female was to become a cornerstone of religious law as written in the New Testament. If a woman is treacherous by her nature, obviously she needs to be under the direct control and subjugation of a man. Institutionalization of this idea was to become a reality when Apostle Paul wrote, "for the man is not of the woman; but the woman of the man. Neither was the man created for the woman; but the woman for the man" (I Corinthians 11:8, 9).

Subjugation and control of women were not the sole concern of western religious thinkers. Quoting from the Hindu Code of Manu No. 5 (circa 100 A.D.), "in childhood, woman must be subject to her father, in youth to her husband, and when her husband is dead, to her sons. A woman must never be free of subjugation" (Aphra, 1972, p. 48).

The male privileges of subjugation and control were often enforced with physical chastisement. Nor was it unusual for the chastisement to end in her death. Constantine I, the first Christian Emperor of Rome, had his young wife Fausta boiled to death in vat. Other secular and religious leaders, though somewhat less extreme, used force to rule over their wives. Martin Luther admitted he beat his wife, the former nun, Katherine, when she talked back to him; (Davidson, 1977). William the Conqueror raped a young woman in order to force their marriage which she did not want (Brownmiller, 1975). King Henry VIII was notorious for the number of wives he had murdered.

During the Middle Ages violence between husband and wife was prevalent among the general populace as well as the gentry, prompting Bernard of Sienna, in 1427, to ask his male parishioners to treat their wives with as much mercy as they did their pigs and other animals under their care. Abbe de Brantome in the 16th century wrote to Christian lords and princes deploring the freedom with which they murdered their wives, noting that the pagans had been more gentle to their

5

wives than they (Davis, 1971).

The voices of reason and compassion were not unopposed. In 1521, Justice Brooke insisted that it was acceptable to beat one's wife as it was to beat a "traitor, pagan or villain" (Gayford, 1977a, p. 122). During the reign of Charles II (1660-4685) English Common Law was codified into an act which permitted wife beating as a form of chastisement. The codification of French Common Law occurred during the reign of Napolean between 1800 and 1804. It was his view that woman were to be considered "legal minors their entire lives" (Davidson, 1977, p. 15). A common saying of that day was that "women, like walnut trees should be beaten every day" (Davidson, 1977, p. 14).

The Russian culture, likewise, had its version of these laws.

> In Russia during the reign of Ivan the Terrible in the 16th century, the state church sanctified the oppression of women by issuing a Household Ordinance that spelled out when and how a man might most effectively beat his wife. A man was even permitted to kill a wife or a serf if he did so for disciplinary purposes. (Mandel, cited in Martin, 1976, p. 30)

In England, beatings were so common in some districts, they were known by the manner of beating administered there. Liverpool was known as the "kicking district" because the husbands kicked their wives with hobnailed boots (Gayford, 1977a).

It was not until the passage of the Matrimonial Causes Act of 1857, the Woman's Property Act of 1882, and the Matrimonial Causes Act of 1884 that woman achieved emancipation. These rulings followed on the heels of the 1855 law which make it no longer legal in Britain for a husband to sell his wife or daughter into prostitution if she were under 16 years old. In 1878, it became legally possible for a battered wife to leave her husband if he had been convicted of abuse. In 1891, British husbands could no longer keep their wives under lock and key (Gayford, 1977b).

America was greatly influenced by Sir William Blackstone who wrote in his Commentaries of the Law of England (1765-1769) that it was reasonable for a husband to beat his wife.

6

For, as (the husband) is to answer for her misbehavior, the law thought it reasonable to intrust him with this power of chastisement, in the same moderation that a man is allowed to correct his apprentices or children. (Davidson, 1977, p. 19)

Many states enacted early laws condoning wife abuse, many of which remained until the end of the 19th century. Prior to 1874, in North Carolina, it was acceptable for a man to beat his wife with a switch no bigger than his thumb. It was also legal in Mississippi, until 1894, for a husband to chastise his wife with a whip. In Pennsylvania husbands were prohibited from beating their wives after 10 P.M. or on Sunday.

In recent years, the problem of wife abuse has received attention throughout the world. France outlawed wifebeating in 1924. Scotland and Iran passed similar laws in the 1970's; Brazil made it illegal for husbands to sell, rent, or gamble away their wives. Italy outlawed wifebeating i 1975, though before that time it had been the husband's right under the Roman law of Patris Potestas (Martin, 1976).

Unfortunately, attitudes are less readily changeable than the law. In a recent edition of The Fresno Bee, a California newspaper, there appeared a syndicated cartoon in which a husband, away on a hunting trip with friends, gambles away his wife. The husband, speaking to her on the telephone said; "Yeah honey, the hunting's been great. . . Oh, by the way, you now belong to Herb Haskins." Clearly, women are still regarded as property (Foreman & Templeton, The Fresno Bee, 1978, p. D5).

Another recent example comes from Japan:

Eisaku Sato, former Prime Minister of Japan was awarded the Nobel Peace Prize in 1974. Prior to his nomination for the award, Sato's wife had accused him publicly of beating her. . . Sato's popularity skyrocketed after his wife revealed: Yes, he's a good husband, he only beats me once a week. (Martin, 1976, p. 45)

Overview

7

The last section of this chapter provides a brief overview of the chapters that will follow. Chapter 2 examines the battered woman, with an emphasis on her early childhood and its consequences for interpersonal relationships and her self-image. Evidence for a "battered wife syndrome" is examined.

In Chapter 3 the attitudes and behavior of the violent husband are explored, and "neurotic pride" is posited as the nearly universal trait which leads to "conjugal terrorism."

In Chapter 4 the husband-wife interaction and the cyclical pattern of the violent episode are described. The chapter also examines the community response to "conjugal terrorism."

In Chapter 5 models for two programs to assist battered women are presented. The first is a shelter for physical safety, while the second program offers job training and peer counseling to help promote independent functioning.

In Chapter 6 the rationale for a community approach to wife abuse is demonstrated and recommendations for further research and programs are offered.

CHAPTER 2

THE BATTERED WIFE

It has only been in the last 10 years, with the development of the women's movement, that the issue of physical abuse of woman has received the attention of the mental health profession. Since the development of successful treatment approaches to the problems of the rape victim, people are demanding services for abused women. However, because violence against women is such an integral part of the American culture (Straus, 1976), wife abuse has not been defined as a problem.

Relatively little is known about battered women due to the lack of research and writing on the subject. Demonstrating this avoidance, neither the national nor state psychological conventions in the past two years has included workshops on wife abuse or family violence.

> Prior to 1971, violent family members were among the missing persons in family research. No articles whose titles contained the word violence had appeared in the <u>Journal of Marriage and the Family</u> before the special issue on violence in November 1971. (Gelles & Straus, 1978, p. 1)

Investigations of conjugal violence are being carried out at three different levels: (a) demographic, (b) sociological, and (c) psychological. Demographic information is being collected at shelters, in clinical programs, and by university researchers. Sociological investigations is looking at how the culture reinforces and supports conjugal violence, how conjugal violence is transmitted from generation to generation, and how our folklore, literature, and media support violence toward women (Gelles & Straus, 1978). Psychological research is looking to find the bases for the attitudes and behavior of abused women and their violent husbands. Psychologists are also seeking the connection between early childhood experience of parental abuse and subsequent episodes of wife abuse.

A number of researchers (Ball, 1977; Carlson, 1977; Gayford, 1975; Gelles, 1976; Prescott & Letko, 1977) have assembled a constellation of attitudes and characteristics that describe the battered wife. This configuration of background history, values, and behaviors has been coined "the battered wife syndrome" by Star (1978).

The Battered Wife Syndrome

The early emotional life of the battered woman was full of disruptions. The emotional atmosphere was restrictive and usually lacked warmth and affections. She was not allowed to express strong feelings. She was often instructed never to talk back, and not to be angry. During her teenage years she was not allowed to date or act independently.

These experiences helped isolate her from her peers, and she became a "loner," with few friends or social contacts. These constricting events undermined her self-esteem, and her lack of understanding contributed to her sense of low self-worth. Not surprisingly, when she dated she tended to become pregnant, or marry early to escape her family. Lacking social experience, she married a man who appeared to be strong and protective, but who in actually was emotionally rigid and sexually repressed. They both held very traditional views about sex role identification.

Socially the couple remained isolated (Star, 1978). They used each other as the sole definer of cultural norms and rarely included others in their decision-making processes. All major decisions were made by the husband. The wife often was not provided money of her own, not allowed the use of a car, nor allowed to visit outside the home. On the few occasions that they went out socially, it was to go drinking with his friends.

The violence usually began during the first year of marriage. Her attempts at finding help were often thwarted by family and professional care-providers. She was often made to feel as if she were the cause of the violence and not the victim. Over the course of time, low self-esteem combined with the stress of the violence made it almost impossible for her to focus her psychic strength on problem solving. She seemed to run from one solution to the next without success. When she was injured there was only a 50% chance she would see medical assistance (Star, 1978).

Several studies have contributed to the present understanding for the battered wife. These studies suggest the complexity of variables that should be considered when describing the battered wife.

In a study of 58 women comparing battered to non-battered, both living at a shelter for abused women in southern California, Star (1978) used the following: a background questionnaire, the Buss-Durkee Hostility-Guilt Inventory, and Cattell 16-PF and 1-hour clinical interview. Her results showed that:

> Battered women tended to be less educated... both battered women and their spouses tended to be affiliated with the Catholic religion... the battered women in this study repressed anger, were timid, emotionally reserved, and had lower coping abilities. They showed no signs of being submissive people, instead they scored within the normal balance of the submissive-assertive continuum. These factors point to passivity rather than masochism. They often perceived themselves unable to effect change in their environments. (pp. 16-17)

In a similar study, although without the comparison group, Star, Clark, Goetz, and O'Malia (1978) described a "battered woman profile."

> The overall profile depicts women with low self-esteem, a lack of self-confidence, and a tendency to withdraw. The women displayed an aloof quality, a critical or uncompromising attitude, and a sense of discomfort when interacting with others. The combination of shyness and reserve generally reflects traits developed in childhood as a result of poor

11

early life relationships. The women are also anxious and have trouble binding their anxiety. The test results reveal an emotionality or sensitivity that leaves them feeling easily hurt, frustrated, perturbed and overwhelmed. (p. 10)

Ball (1977) described the women in her study as bewildered and helpless. They were very dependent, with feeling of low self-esteem. To the extent that they exhibited masochistic tendencies, these were related to early childhood experiences of abuse and neglect. They felt they had once loved their husbands and wanted them changed. They identified strongly with their marital role and were unable to comtemplate leaving.

Gayford (1975), who studied 100 battered women in England, reported that the women, as well as their husbands, had been brought up in families of conflict and violence. Less than two thirds of the women were brought up by both parents until the age of 15. Almost one quarter experienced violence regularly in their parental homes. Two thirds did not complete their schooling, and 69% were pregnant out of wedlock.

In a study of 38 battered women conducted by prescott and Letko (1977), the women filled out a self-report questionnaire which showed that 10% had been beaten as children. Thirty percent of the women reported that their husbands had been beaten as children. Twenty-four women, or 63%, reported their parents fought regularly. Of those women with children, 43% felt that the violence may have affected the children's attitudes toward marriage in general. The daughters were fearful of men and distrustful of intimate relationships.

The mothers of these children reported feeling angry and resentlful in 90% of the cases. A survey of these women's attitudes revealed that 68% felt trapped while 55% felt helpless and 75% felt depressed. From a quarter to a third of the women felt humilated, inadequate, or guilty. These feeling, in addition to the violence itself, resulted in poor sexual adjustment for 73% of them. Seventy-five percent admitted a general distrust of men.

Gelles (1976), studying 80 families, found that 66% of the women who had seen abuse between their parents, grew up to be beaten ` as adults. Carlson (1977), in her study of 260 female victims over an 18-

12

month period, found that one third of the victims and one half of the assailants observed violence between their parents. She also found several common characteristics among the women:

1. They suffered from extremely low self-esteem.
2. They felt socially isolated.
3. They had an intense attachment to their children.

The last study was an effort to understand the battered women by examining both the husband and the wife (Snell, Rosenwald, & Roby, 1964), and these cases were exceptional in that the husbands were brought to trial for their violence. The researchers concluded that the wives were "aggressive, efficient, masculine, and sexually frigid," while the husbands were "shy, sexually ineffectual, reasonably hard working mother's boys with a tendency to drink excessively" (p. 111). The Snell et al. (1964) study is also unique in that its findings are dissimilar to other studies mentioned above raising the question of the relativity of social perception.

> What men describe as aggressiveness in females, women see as asserting their personal integrity; when men automatically see as masculinity in females, women sense as their competence. What some men may see as frigidity, appears to women to be a natural lack of sexual responsiveness to their violent husbands. And what men see as masochism, women report as the sense of being trapped inside their marriages. (Prescott & Letko, 1977, p. 73)

In summary, it has been seen that battered women are a diverse group whose problems are complex and deep seated. Although independent researchers have chosen to highlight various aspects of the problem, certain characteristics recur. These characteristics are that the women: (a) have extremely low self-esteem, (b) feel responsible for the violence in many cases, (c) have learned to be helpless and unable to do things for themselves, and (d) are socially isolated. Understanding the psychosocial makeup of the battered wife combined with other factors makes comprehensible

13

the reasons the woman stays.

Why the Wife Remains in the Relationship

Three levels of analysis are needed when attempting to answer why a battered woman stays in the violent relationship (Gelles, 1976). There are political, cultural, and psychological levels which operate simultaneously.

From a political perspective husbands are in a position of power because they control the family resources. Battered wives are often kept virtual prisoners in their own homes by the lack of money and the lack of access to a car. Often their husbands will not let them hold a job or have personal friends. This ensures her economic dependence and his position of dominance. At the same time there are not resources available within the community for battered wives. The vast majority of battered women have limited job skills and have no way to expand their areas of interest or abilities. Local schools do not have day care facilities and even the minimal tuition at most state colleges is too much for their meager budgets.

In addition to the lack of resources, these women must contend with the cultural and historical stereotypes which dictate who they should behave. When a battered wife approaches her family or friends she is often told she must "stick it out for the sake of the kids." There is also the feeling, "you've make your bed so lie in it." The battered woman is also reminded that "marriage is the woman's responsibility." These homilies attempt to reinforce the notion that the woman must bear any burden if she is to have a man to care for her. As one woman put it, "any man is better than no man."

Reinforcing this desperate position is the fact that women have not been financially able to care for themselves and their children. Traditionally, pay scales are inadequate while lack of training programs and social disapproval of business and career asperations for women have reinforced their financial passivity.

From the psychological perspective, some battered women appear to fall into the syndrome of "learned helplessness."[1] These women have been physically and psychologically terrorized into submission, intimidated by their past experiences. Seligman (1976), who termed

14

this phenomenon "learned helplessness," discovered that, if you imprison a dog in a cage and administer painful electric shocks through the grid in the floor while preventing his escape, the animal will eventually give up trying to escape. When you open the cage and allow him to escape, he will not leave. Seligman explained the effects of his experiments:

> These uncontrolled events can significantly debilitate men and animals. They can produce passivity in the face of trauma, inability to learn that responding is effective, and emotional stress and depression. In short, exposure to uncontrollable events produces a reaction that can be characterized as helplessness. (Seligman, 1976, p. 2)

The traumatic effects of imprisonment in a shocking situation caused the animal to forget that it could leave an open cage. In order to re-train it, Seligman had to drag the animal through the open door several times before it understood escape was possible. It is hypothesized that this same mechanism may be working with battered women who are trapped in destructive relationships with no escape possible.

Other women stay in the violent relationship because they were taught that it was the man's right to beat his wife and that this was a sign of affection. There are many ideological subgroups in this country who still believe it is the husband's duty to chastise his wife in order to teach her her place. These women are taught their place in the family by seeing violence in their parental home. They were often abused as children (Gayford, 1975; Prescott & Letko, 1977).

There are other women who stay because they have such a low opinion of themselves that they will accept any fate that befalls them. These women suffer from what the writer has termed "neurotic acceptance." The women feel worthless and have an extremely difficult time saying "No!" even when their personal safety is at stake. They have literally abandoned their civil and

---

¹
The writer has since learned that this concept has been applied to battered women by another investigator (Walker, 1979). The present conceptualization was arrived at independently.

15

personal rights in the face of physical and psychological trauma. They appear to be unable to think critically for fear that it might be considered a form of rebellion. These women should not be confused with those who are masochistic; they are not looking for violence as a way to work out their negative self-image, but rather feel that if this is what they have this is what they deserve.

Finally, there are those women who stay because they are masochistic. These women are symbolically acting out behavior developed while infants and children relating to their parents.

> Masochism means loving a person who gives hate and ill treatment. The subject relives and re-enacts in inter-personal relations a submissive devotion to a need for the love of a hating or rejecting love object who was originally a parent of his childhood who lives in his superego. It is the superego that keeps the original situation alive through transference to any suitable person or set of circumstances in later life. (Berliner, 1947, p. 469)

The masochistic relationship develops because the dependent child is not in a position of power to demand its right to have love. The child is unable to exercise its option to leave the unrewarding relationship it is is to survive. The child submits and accepts the suffering as if it were love and represses awareness of the pain. The fear of losing the parental love object is so great, and the love so total, the child exonerates the parent and says in effect, "I am the bad one, not you" (Berliner, 1958). Masochism becomes the solution to the infant's conflict over receiving pain in place of love.

In order to get back the love that is withheld by the parent, the child submits to further abuse, experiencing a wish to be purified by the pain and in this way to become worthy of love. The suffering means that the "self" is worthy of bing loved and this pleases the child. There is a feeling of righteousness to the suffering, leaving the person feeling she would rather be right than happy.

In wanting to please the parent, the child may act out the hating parent's view of the child's unworthiness. She may regress to less successful moded

16

of adaptation, thus failing at her tasks. She may choose less demanding goals and underachieve. She may give up hope of succeeding in life an stop trying altogether. These solutions all result from and express a feeling of powerlessness (May, 1972).

This concludes the discussion of some possible reasons why a battered wife might stay in a violent relationship. Chapter 2 has presented the "battered wife syndrome" and her psychogenesis. As can be seen in Figure 1, early emotional trauma leads to a neurotic willingness to uncritically accept one's fate, which in truth leads to the condition of learned helplessness. In this condition one forgets how to protect oneself from attack because one feels powerless. The chapter concluded with a review of some possible explanations of why the battered wife stays including political, cultural, and psychological.

The next chapter will broaden the focus of conjugal violence by looking at the characteristics of the violent husband. The chapter will present several theories of human violence and in conjunction with what is known about violent husbands from clinical research, present a framework from which "conjugal terrorism" can be understood.

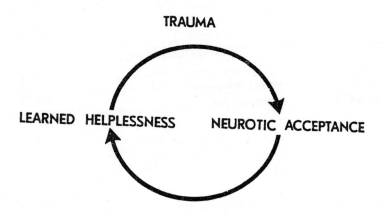

Figure 1. Psychogenesis of the battered wife.

CHAPTER 3

THE VIOLENT HUSBAND

This chapter reviews the literature about the behavior and attitudes of violent husbands. Several theories of human aggression will be examined as potential determinant of their behavior, although no single theory appears adequate in explaining wife abuse. Thus, there is a need for a theoretical orientation that integrates these different theories with the behavior of these men. The last section of this chapter proposes a model of "conjugal terrorism" which attempts to present an intergrative view of abuse.

Characteristics of the Violent Husband

There have been a number of attempts to classify the temperaments, behavior, and ontogenesis of violent husbands. The next section surveys the extent of pathology, their emotional needs, interpersonal demands, and childhood experiences.

The Question of Pathology

Steinmetz denies that men who beat their wives are psychologically deviant from the rest of society. "Most of the studies have shown that they are not psychologically ill. In most respects, they would be like anyone else. This might be called the psychopathology myth" (Steinmetz in Langley & Levy, 1977, p. 49).

Steinmetz proposed that these men could be categorized according to the way in which they resolve their conflicts. These types are the screaming slugger, the threatener, the silent attacker, and the pacifist.

The first of these four types, the "screaming slugger," is both verbally and physically assaultive. The second type, the "threatener," is more verbally than physically assaultive. The third type, the "silent attacker," explodes without warning. The last, the "pacifist," withdraws from conflict.

Unlike Steinmetz, Shainess (1977) believes the violent husband's behavior is pathological in nature. Based on her clinical experience, Shainess proposed six categories to describe violent husbands. These are: (a) passive-aggressive, (b) obsessive-compulsive, (c) sadistic, (d) brute, (e) infantile, and (f) jealous.

The "passive-aggressive" male tends to feel helpless and vulnerable, and becomes enraged when threatened with loss of an emotionally valued object or possession. The "obsessive-compulsive" male needs to feel he has control over his environment and tends to explode under the stress of perceived loss of control. The "sadistic" male is purposely out to destroy his partner. The "brute" insists on using intimidation to resolve all differences. The "infantile" male has a limited ability to tolerate frustration and limited impulse control. The "jealous" male fears other men will steal his wife away from him because he is undeserving of her love.

Interpersonal Dynamics

Wife abusers can also be characterized in terms of their inter-personal needs and demands. In a study of 23 men who seriously assaulted their spouses or partners, Faulk (1974) found five types of abusing relationships. These included the: (a) passive-dependent, (b) dependent-suspicious, (c) violent-bully, (d) dominating, and (e) stable and affectionate.

First were the "passive-dependent" who were trying to please and to passify their demanding mates. Frustration accumulated and the violence reduced the tension. The next were the "dependent-suspicious" men with long histories of overt suspicion of their wives' fidelity, but with a strong need to stay in the relationship. Tension built up over time and was reduced by violence. The next were the "violent-bullying" men who used violence and intimidation to get what they wanted. Alcohol abuse was often associated with their violence. Fourth were the "dominating" husbands who needed to assert themselves to prove their power. They became violent when they thought their power was threatened. The last type was the "stable and affectionate" man who became violent during a period of mental disturbance, usually involving severe depression.

Emotional Needs

Elbow (1977) divided the husbands she studied into four categories according to the core emotional resources needed by each husband. These were labeled: (a) controller, (b) defender, (c) approval-seeker, and (d) incorporator.

The "controller" has a strong need for autonomy and sees himself as controlling himself by controlling others. In so doing, he does not experience self-control but depends upon strong external controls which he resents and sees as ineffectual. The second, the "defender," has a strong need for protection, and experiences fear of being harmed when his desires conflict with internal or external limits. He strikes out before he is struck, and like the controller, has a tendency to feel self-righteous. The third, the "approval-seeker," equates approval of his beliefs and actions with confirmation of his worth as a person. He has only a weak sense of himself as worthy and if challenged loses faith in himself. He becomes violent when confronted verbally or when his perceptions are questioned. Finally, the "incorporator" desperately needs affirmation to validate his sense of being a whole person. Because he needs to incorporate his wife's ego for his sense of wholeness, he tends to see himself as reflected in his wife's behavior. If she is good, so is he. He keeps his wife as a virtual prisoner, rarely allowing her to visit others or have close friends of her own. Threatened with her loss, he becomes violent.

Common psychological profiles in the interactions of violent men were found by Elbow (1977). The men refused to take responsibility for their behavior, blaming their wives for the marital violence which they claimed resulted from her "nagging." They could not tolerate their wives' autonomy, feeling that any deviation from their strict control threatened their well-being. These women were not allowed to hold jobs, continue their education, or pursue outside interests. As the men considered the relationship with their wives symbolic of the one they had with their mothers, the wives were expected to perform duties and respond to their husbands in ways imitating the men's mothers.

Fear of intimacy is another common characteristic of violent husbands. They had rigid expectations of marriage and sex-role behavior, and demanded strict adherence to them. These men could not tolerate intimacy and this showed up most vividly in their poor sex lives. Violence was a defense against the intimacy they feared (Kardener & Fuller, 1970).

Early Ontogenesis

The major characteristics of violent men appear in childhood. In her study of family violence, Ball (1977) discovered that the violent husbands had a long history of explosive tempers and fighting. This pattern often appeared during adolescence. These men often overreacted to being slighted or ridiculed and were unskilled in relating to others.

Ball found that these men had violent childhoods where their parents abused them and each other. The fathers were characterized as punitive and strict authoritarians. They had a history of fighting and assaultive behavior, and violence was learned as a way of dealing with interpersonal problems. A loss of one or both of their parents typically occurred in childhood, while social isolation and financial hardship were predominant in their lives. Violent impulses seemed to be generated by the threat of loss which served to reenforce their feelings of low self-esteem, inadequacy, and a sense of impotence and helplessness.

In order to further understand the violent husband's behavior, general theories of human aggression and violence will be reviewed. Although they will not fully explain why a man will beat his wife, they attempt to explain why a man becomes violent in a variety of situations.

Theories of Violence

There are many different theories of human aggression and violence (Gelles & Straus, 1978; Wedge, 1977). The order to understand the complex nature of

22

the violent relationship several theoretical orientations are presented. These approaches include ethology, ecology, physiology, and psychology.

Graver (1968) pointed out that the meaning of violence extends beyond the physical act. "It is important to recognize that the concept of violence is a moral concept, and that the moral elements come in through the fact an act of violence is a violation of a person" (p. 12). Violence, to Garver, is the interaction of physical and psychological elements. "Psychological violence . . . involves manipulating people. It often involves degrading people. "It often involves a kind of terrorism" (Garver, 1968, p. 8). This definition adds a psychological component to the explanation. Gelles (1976) and Straus (1974) limit the definition of violence to a physical plane, making it synonymous with physical aggression. Aggression may be on the continuum ranging from assertion to violence, however, without a psychological component, such a definition has limited value to the study of violent husbands.

Ethological Theory

This theory proposes that there is an inborn releaser that makes all animals, including humans, act violently when their territory is invaded or threatened with invasion (Ardrey, 1966; Lorena, 1966). Leakey and Lewin (1977) extend the theory in the following manner:

Humans are aggressive...because there is a universal territorial instinct in biology; territories are established and maintained by displays of aggression; our ancestors acquired weapons, turning ritual displays into bloody combat, a development that was exacerbated through a lust for killings. (p. 58)

Ethological theory is an extension of the Darwinian concept of survival of the fittest as modified by Spencer into the social survival of the strong. Hornstein (1976) reminds us that the explanation may be more complicated than Lorenz would have us believe, after all, "genes create potential . . . they do not determine social patterns" (p. 1).

23

Ecological Theory

Territory is not only physical space. Hall (1966) proposed that humans have an invisible boundary surrounding them which he called "personal space." Personal space can be broken down into four zones, each a certain distance from the body. Personal space acts as a form of territory and protects the person's sense of privacy. Privacy is important to emotional development because it promotes separation and individuation (Chapin, 1951; Jourard, 1966; Kira, 1966).

Even more private and intimate than personal space is "psychological space" (Bakker & Bakker-Rabdau, 1973). Psychological space is the psychological territory people maintain in their relationships with others. It is "the total amount of influence which each person exerts over the thoughts and feelings of all the individuals present" (p. 18). When a man's psychological space is violated he becomes hostile. Hostility is "behavior which seeks to destroy or injure an individual or his territory. . . it results from a person's inability to defend his territory" (p. 63).

As privacy promotes human well-being, "crowding" acts in destructive ways. The consequences of crowding are pathological behaviors (Calhoun, 1962; Christina, Flyger, & Davis, 1960; Franklin & Mitchell, 1973; Galle, Grove, & McPherson, 1972).

"Crowding" is an interpersonal process that results from having more interaction that one can tolerate. In studies of human environments, population density has been found to correlate highly with juvenile delinquency and adult crime (Bordua, 1958; Lander, 1954; Schmitt, 1957). Positive correlations between mental illness and density have also been reported (Faris & Durham, 1965; Lantz, 1953; Queen, 1948).

Physiological Theory

Neurological research with humans and laboratory animals has found that lesions in the temporal lobe of the limbic system cause explosive rage known as "temporal-lobe" epilepsy or "psychomotor seizures." In humans it is thought to be the most frequent organic cause of human violence (Elliot, 1977). Elliot described the characteristics as:

24

Frequent episodes of intense rage which are
triggered by trivial irritations and are
accompanied by verbal or physical violence.
Speech his explosive and marked by unwanted
obscenities and profanity. The violence
itself has a primitive quality - biting,
gouging, kicking, spitting, multiple stabbing
and so on. A small number of patients also
exhibit poor impulse control in sexual
matters, which lead to sexual assaults.
Pathological intoxication is common; a small
amount of alcohol either triggers an attack
of rage or produces drunkenness. (1977, pp.
104-105)

Some biological research has uncovered an
abnormality in the chromosonal makeup of violent men
that produces a readiness to act violently. The
abnormality is the presence of an additional Y
chromosome in the pair responsible for the person's
gender. Increased levels of aggressive behavior are
thought to come from the resultant "hyper-masculinity"
(Goldstein, 1975; Jacobs, Brunton, & Melville, 1965).
It has been proposed, in addition, that violence
is caused by a disorder of the metabolic process.
Hypoglycemia has been found to cause explosive rage.
The relationship, however is not that straightforward:

The fact that rage is not induced by the
hypoglycemia which can occur during a five-
hour glucose-tolerance test, even in people
who have hypoglycemic reactions outside the
laboratory, emphasizes the role for the
social setting. (Wilder, in Elliot, 1977, p.
103)

Psychological Theories

Violence may be learned through imitation of
modeling (Bandura, Ross, & Ross, 1961; Singer, 1971),
where in addition to patterns of behavior one accepts
the norms that violence is approved (Owens & Straus,
1975). Recent research and analysis seem to support
these conclusions (Gelles, 1973; Gil, 1971; Steele &
Polleck, 1974).
Evidence from the histories of violent husbands
appear to support the idea that violence is learned.

25

Levine (1975) found that 74% of the husbands he studied came from violent homes. Flynn (1977) reported that 40% of his sample were beaten as children. Eisenberg and Micklow (1974) found that 50% of the husbands they studied experienced violence in their parental homes. Prescott and Letko (1977) found 30% of their sample had been beaten as children.

Frustration-aggression theorists proposed that frustration always precedes a violent act and makes the individual predisposed to violence (Dollard, Doob, Miller, Mower, & Sears, 1939). It appears that frustration develops as important life goals are blocked by someone or something. The frustrated person will then either attack directly what is blocking him, or attack a less threatening target, thus displacing his aggression.

Other theorists have postulated that it is the frustration of early dependency needs of the infant that predisposes humans to act aggressively (Maslow, 1962; May, 1972). Studies with laboratory animals have reached similar conclusions (Gray, 1971; Harlow, 1974).

According to psychodynamic theory (Horney, 1950), what appears to happen in young children is that as a result of their early feelings of omnipotence, frustration of dependency needs produce intense feelings of rage. The child, frightened by the power of his rage, imagines his parents will destroy or abandon him to rid themselves of his anger. To prevent this catastrophe, the child deflects his anger onto himself.

Feelings of abandonment make the child believe he is powerless and this produces depression. By mobilizing the anger and acting violently the child combats deep feelings of despair that come from his sense of helplessness. Feeling of helplessness and despair have been reported associated with violence (King, 1975; May, 1972).

Some researchers believe that violence is used to ward off feared intimate experiences (Kardener & Fuller, 1970). Violent husbands fearing intimacy in their marriages may beat their wives to control their fears. They feared intimate relationships because the ones they had with their parents were disastrous. Spiegel (1967) wrote that violence often covers up deep-seated feelings of depression which were associated with early experiences of abandonment by a loved one. The violence was a form of revenge for the resentment following the feeling of abandonment.

26

Human violence may also be viewed from an interactional model of psychopolitics. Psychopolitics is the interplay of psychological motives and political decisions. From this perspective, "violence" is defined as a political act designed to deny the victim this personal and civil rights by violating this personal and psychological space. Violence is used to maintain the position of power one individual has over the other. Power accrues to the person controlling the resources. Political decisions involve establishing how resources are to be controlled and distributed.

Gelles (1976), studying 41 cases of wife beating, found that the fewer the resources a wife had, the more likely she was to remain in a violent relationship. It appears that one's physical safety and psychological well-being is affected by whether or not one has access to resources.

Violence may also erupt either because it is inevitable in human relationships (Dahrendorf, 1968) or because all social systems rely on violence to further their objectives (Goode, 1971) proposed that people tend to become violent when they feel they have been treated unjustly or have not been adequately compensated for their efforts.

These have been but a few of the many theories that account for human aggression, and none is sufficient to fully explain why a husband beats and terrorizes his wife. The next section will attempt to draw together what has been presented into a more comprehensive theoretical orientation. It will focus on the concept of "neurotic pride" and its role in developing "conjugal terrorism."

Neurotic Pride

Men who murder their wives often have a long history of violence dating back to adolescence. One researcher who interviewed nine teenage murderers concluded that they have very strong feelings of omnipotence (King, 1975). King believed that the omnipotence was largely the result of the youths' inability to communicate their needs or desires. The youths could not tolerate reasoning and lacked verbal fluency. They were then forced to rely on their feelings to put order into their world and in the process became over-reliant on these inner cues. The results was exaggerated feelings of self-importance.

Other researchers studying the personality development of murderers proposed that they suffered from "neurotic pride" (Ruotolo, 1975; Yachnes, 1975). Neurotic pride was a concept first promulgated by Horney (1950) and refers to a person's belief in an idealized self-image. The idealized self-image is felt to exist independently of the person's other personality characteristics. Neurotic pride substitutes for the real self-confidence the person lacks, and serves to reduce anxiety while providing an acceptable identity.

According to Horney, neurotic pride develops in part because of the individual's alienation from his or her feelings of self-esteem. Under favorable circumstances a person will strive toward maturity by seeking his personal growth and emotional fulfillment through interpersonal relationships.

> But through a variety of adverse influences, a child may not be permitted to grow according to his individual needs and possibilities. As a result, the child does not develop a feeling of belonging, of we, but instead a profound insecurity and vague apprehensiveness . . . basic anxiety. (Horney, 1950, p. 18)

Basic anxiety leaves the young child feeling alone and in danger of attack with no apparent means of protection. "The cramping pressure of his basic anxiety prevents the child from relating himself to others with the spontaneity of his real feelings and forces him to find ways to cope with them" (Horney, 1950, p. 18)

The child's attempts at coping take the form of moving toward others in a clinging and compliant manner, moving against others in an aggressive or hostile manner, or moving away from them by emotionally withdrawing. These moves are rigid and extreme and are exhibited with an intensity that is proportional to the amount of basic anxiety present.

Under these circumstances, the child is driven in many directions at once. This reduces interpersonal effectiveness and results in a fundamental contradictory attitude toward interpersonal relations. This constitutes the child's basic conflict with others, Horney believed. In an attempt to resolve the conflict, the child selects one movement to predominate.

For many reasons, he has not had the chance to develop real self-confidence: his inner strength has been sapped by his having to be on the defensive, by his being divided, by the way in which his early solution initiated a one-sided development, thereby making large areas of his personality unavailable for constructive uses. Hence, he desperately needs self-confidence, or a substitute for it. (Horney, 1950, pp. 20-21)

The result of the interplay between basic anxiety and basic conflict is that the person feels ill-equipped to handle the complexities of life.

If he had a sense of belonging, his feeling inferior to others would not be so serious a handicap. But living in a competitive society, and feeling at the bottom . . . isolated and hostile, he can only develop an urgent need to lift himself above others. (Horney, 1950, p. 21)

In order to regain a feeling of identity and importance, the alienated man creates an idealized image of himself. He tries to live up to the image he offers to others as a substitute for his real self. The reliance on a false image underlies the neurotic pride core, further covered up with additional layers of false belief and behaviors. The result of this is that the person lives under constant tension, fearful of exposure, and ready to explode at any moment (Yachnes, 1975).

At the center of the murderer's personality is a core of neurotic pride, itself, mixed with a component of self-hate so explosive that any threat to its stability, such as a challenge to the person's position of power or dominance, results in violence or murder (Ruotolo, 1975). Rapid penetration of this inner core by circumstances is intolerable, and demands retaliation.

Many violent husbands appear to be struggling with their unresolved feelings about unmet dependency needs unconsciously carried into adult life from unhappy childhoods. These men may fear emotional intimacy, since letting to emotionally is seen as surrender or

29

regression to a vulnerable infantile state. Loss of control is frequently equated with going "crazy." Underneath this issue may be the men's struggle for emotional individuation.

During early childhood many of the men who subsequently beat their wives found themselves competing with their fathers for the emotional attention, support, and nurturance of their mother. Their fathers also had unresolved dependency needs and saw their sons as a threat to the source of motherly succor they felt they needed. The wife and mother, drained from this conflict, was forced to withdraw emotionally for self-protection. The child felt the competition and the abandonment, but was forced to tolerate it because he was powerless to change it. However, the child carried the seeds of unconscious resentment, secretly hoping for revenge. It is this reverent motif that keeps him tied to his original family.

As an adult the violent husband may not have worked through his early dependency needs and tries to deny them by dominating others. His neurotic pride demands that he always be in control of his feelings. He is rigid and emotionally repressed and sees his wife as a threat because she is free to express her feelings and is open about her dependency needs. In order to control his fears he feels he must dominate and control her behavior. He resents his dependency needs which leave him vulnerable and resents his wife because she embodies those qualities he cannot tolerate in himself.

It is at this junction between the neurotic drive for supremacy of his idealized self-image and his need to dominate and control his wife's behavior that the violent husband often becomes the "conjugal terrorist."

Conjugal Terrorism

Conjugal terrorism is a term describing the behavior of the violent husband, whose attitudes and behavior bear a remarkable resemblance to those of the political terrorist. Conjugal terrorism is the use or threatened use of violence in order to break down the resistance of the victim to the will of the terrorist. It is "the use of coercive intimidation for political motives" (Wilkinson, 1974, p. 11). Ultimately the terrorist uses violence to further his political cause and for the conjugal terrorist, the violent husband, his political cause is the maintenance of his idealized self-image.

The conjugal terrorist, like the political terrorist, feels he is morally superior to those he associates with. As the political terrorists has a vision of world or political order and a sense of what is "right" or "good," the conjugal terrorist likewise believes he must assume the moral responsibility for his wife. He often says he needs to teach her a lesson or to teach her how to behave properly. Both have a rather narrow and rigid definition of what is "proper" and rely almost entirely on self-contained or inner cues in order to make decisions or judgments. Both have a tenuous sense of their power and are easily frightened. They feel under attack from the environment and use violence to control their fears.

The parallel between the two is not limited to motivation alone. Wilkinson (1974) pointed out the characteristics of political terrorism as: (a) indiscriminant, unpredictable ruthless violence, and (b) the terrorist's amorality. The political terrorist displays an indifference to existing moral codes and believes he is above them. The conjugal terrorist uses indiscriminant, ruthless violence and also feels exempt from the law because the criminal justice system does not make him accountable for his acts.

The violence in either case may be simply an end in itself, or a symbolic act designed to influence political behavior by extranormal means (Thornton, 1964). Jenkins (1975) wrote that the use of violence was for the purpose of effect. The terrorist has a perverse notion of the idea that the ego, or self, is the only reality, and that there is no rule but self-interest (Hymans, 1974)

> The basic idea is to commit an act of sufficient audacity not only to compel attention but to demonstrate beyond doubt the inability of existing authority to prevent its commission or apprehend its perpetrators. (Schreiber, 1978, p. 25)

In either case terrorism is not a philosophy, but a rationalized form of rage. As Parry (1976) wrote, "terrorists feed on problems without solving them" (p. 11). In both instances the men are trying to promote an image of strength and control through intimidation. Analogous to men suffering from "neurotic pride,"

31

terrorist "aim to create an impression of power, invincibility and effectiveness, representing themselves as a force which must inevitably assume supremacy" (Calvery in Wilkinson, 1974, p. 125).

Conclusions

This chapter has presented the findings of researchers working with violent husbands. Their findings and a review of several theories of human violence were pulled together into a conceptual orientation. A model of the psychogenesis of the violent husband, as shown in Figure 2, depicts early emotional trauma leading to neurotic pride as an adjustment and this leading in turn to conjugal terrorism.

The programs proposed in Chapter 5, while designed to reduce the incidence of conjugal terrorism, are not addressed to the needs of violent husbands. The programs deal exclusively with the needs of battered women and their children. This is because:

1. The women are in immediate physical danger and are in crisis.
2. There are no programs for battered women in most cities.
3. The problems of the husband are thought to be too ingrained and longstanding for crisis intervention to be effective.
4. There is great difficulty getting violent husbands to view their behavior as a problem.

Although these programs, which see the women as a population at risk, do not deal directly with the violent husbands, this does not mean they should be denied services. In fact, in Chapter 6 there are recommendations for further research and for initiation of programs through existing or new service delivery systems to work with these men on the basis of community psychology prevention strategies.

The next chapter will round out the picture of conjugal violence by outlining the "cycle of violence" and the community response to the violent episode, with special attention given to the response of the police and the courts.

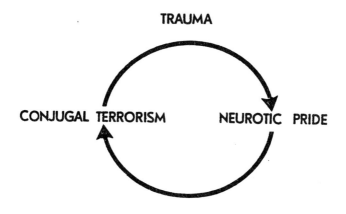

Figure 2. Psychogenesis of the violent husband.

CHAPTER 4

INTERACTIONAL DYNAMICS

The violent episode with its cyclical nature is examined in this chapter. The events can be broken down into three distinct phases, as described below, and intervention strategies appear most adequate when this rhythm is explicitly recognized. Societal involvement in the form of community response to the battered wife is examined as well as factors inhibiting adequate assistance.

Cyclical Pattern

Recognition that there was a cyclical pattern to the incidences of abuse was first proposed by Walker (1979) on the basis of her clinical experience with battered women. Phase I is the tension building phase, Phase II begins with the violent eruption, and Phase III involves attempts at conciliation.

Phase I

The normal events of daily life between the couple causes tension to build up. As the tension rises, the woman senses this and realizes her husband is becoming agitated. At this point she may become nurturing and compliant or decide to stay out of his way. These strategies are aimed at reducing the level of tension he is experiencing. She implicitly accepts his anger as his responsibility, thus allowing her to reduce her anxiety brought abut by the uncertainty of his

34

behavior. If his anger is her fault, she believes, she can change the outcome by behaving differently.

The husband sees her acceptance of responsibility for his anger as an admission of her guilt. This gives him permission to focus his anger on her imagined culpability rather than on his feeling of helplessness in the face of his mounting tension. The woman believes that she is a failure because she has failed in her responsibility to care for her husband, leaving him angry and dissatisfied. As a result of her feelings of failure and hopelessness, she becomes enraged at herself and her husband. She senses that he would destroy her if she expressed her anger openly, so she must deny that it exists.

During Phase I, according to Walker, there may be several occasions where the husband physically and verbally assaults his wife, but these tend to be brief in duration. She begins to withdraw from him and he fears that she will leave him. The fear of abandonment promps him to use violence and threats of violence to intimidate her into staying. Now the tension has reached almost uncontrollable proportions. At this point the woman, unable to function under the mounting pressure and tension, may provoke a blow-up in order to put an end to the unbearable tension and frustration. In this way she attempts to gain psychological control over his violence and the uncertainty of their relationship. Her anxiety is reduced if she knows when to expect the attack.

Phase II

This phase begins with the explosion of violence. At the beginning he may believe his violence is justified and they he is only "teaching her a lesson." To his way of thinking she has transgressed their social contract by provoking him to violence, and now needs to be shown "who's boss." Whatever his motivation in the beginning, his violence is soon out of control. It is not uncommon for him to awaken her from sleep to continue beating her. During the violence he may resort to torture in order to get her to apologize for real or imagined transgressions. At the height of the violence she if often able to dissociate herself from the experience of physical pain so that she is usually able to remember the finer details of the experienced violence. The husband often has a lapse of memory about the specifics of his behavior. This period usually ends within 24 hours.

Phase III

This phase is marked by the husband's feelings of guilt and shame, where he attempts a reconciliation. As with his behavior during other phases, his attempts at conciliation are often overdone. He may shower the woman with gifts and other signs of affection, sometimes coming to her hospital room to beg her forgiveness, vowing never to strike her again. She sees his pleading and gifts as a sign of his underlying love for her. At this time she appears rational and his expressed desire to change sounds believable. He may acknowledge his fears that if she left him he would fall apart. She may believe this to be true as this helps her justify her need to stay with him. In the end she is often swayed not only by his need for reconciliation but by her need to believe she can resurrect his good side. She can continue to believe she is powerful as long as he is willing to let he believe he is willing to change.

Community Involvement

Legal Services

Sometime during either the first or more often the second phase, the battered wife will call upon the police to intervene in her behalf. Many times she will call for the sake of the children rather than for her own safety, but when she calls she is not always assured if or how the police will respond. James Bannon, commander of the Detroit Police Department, admits the following:

> In Detroit, as in many other cities, the treatment of female victims of assault of the domestic variety could charitably be termed cavalier. Not so charitably but perhaps more accurately would be an allegation of misfeasance. (Bannon, 1975, p. 4)

Commander Bannon's candid remarks made to the American Bar Association Convention had not only the advantage of years of experience behind them, but also the benefit of his keen insights. He found that

36

policemen not only failed to protect the woman's rights, thus helping to reduce the violence, but often have made matters worse for their efforts.

It is my view that police and later prosecutors and courts contribute to domestic violence by their Laissez-faire attitudes toward what they view as essentially a personal problem. Further that this view is held because police are socialized to regard females in general as sobordinate. The superordinancy of the male coupled with his socially mandated self-reliance on violence to resolve personal problems without outside assistance assures us that wives will continue to be beaten in record numbers. (Bannon, 1975, p. 4)

What is essentially operating in the police failure to respond adequately to battered women is their attitude. Bannon noted that the police attitude is the direct result of early socialization patterns. Among the factors that contributed to their overall attitude were an overempasis on the ideal of rugged individualism, rather than social interdependence, a view that women are the property of men rather than fully vested citizens, and the notions that marriage is economic dependency coupled with sexual access. He acknowledges:

In my view the police attitude, which seems to say that what happens between man and his wife in their own home is beyond the authority or ability of the police to control, is a cop out. The real reason that the police avoid domestic violence situations to the greatest extent possible is because we do not know how to cope with them, and besides we share society's view that domestic violence is an individual problem and not a public issue. It is amazing to me that we are seemingly unaware of the extreme paradox of delegating to police officers the role of arbiters of family disputes. Of all non-athletic occupations none is so absorbed with the use of physical coersive force as that of police officers. Nor are they any more thoroughly socialized in their masculine role

37

images. This paradox suggests to me that
traditionally trained and socialized
policemen are the worst possible choices to
attempt to intervene in domestic violence.
The known physical propensities may in fact
reinforce the perceived legitimacy of the use
of violence. (Bannon, 1975, pp. 2-3)

Commander Bannon concluded his remarks by
reminding the reader that under the constitution women
were noncitizens. "As such they are not entitled to
the protection extended to fully vested male "citizens"
(p. 9).
In a similiar view, Jackson (1975) observed that
criminal law is basically sexist in its treatment of
women.

The problem . . . is not that women . . .
have no effective remedy within the system as
it now operates. The problem is not a lack
of laws against this sort of activity; there
are many applicable laws . . . The problem is
that these laws, when broken in a family or
quasi-family context, are systematically
unenforced. (p. 1)

Jackson, while recognizing the importance of
historical tradition and socialization, adds an
additional dimension to the understanding of why
battered women are not served by the criminal justice
system.

Perhaps the most cited rationale -- apart
from tradition itself -- for the general
policy of non-enforcement against wife
beating is that complaining wives so often
decide, sometimes as late as the eve of the
trial, not to testify against her husband.
(Jackson, 1975, p. 4)

Jackson pointed out that the very fact that women
failed to prosecute to the fullest extent may be an
artifact of the complex and arduous legal task of
prosecution. Noting the comments of one San Francisco
assistant district attorney, Jackson wrote, "although
in 1973 the Family Bureau received over 5000 calls. . .
only eight . . . led to a complaint and prosecution by
the district attorney's office" (p. 11).

The fact that the criminal justice system often blames the victim (Ryan, 1971) was also pointed out by Bannon in his analysis of 4,900 cases of assault in 1972:

Through the process of conciliation, compliant harassment and prosecutor discretion fewer than 300 of these cases were ultimately tried by a court of law. And in most of these the court used the judicial process to attempt to conciliate rather than adjudicate. If you bear in mind that these cases had been culled over several times so that only where the injury was extreme or the offense repeated would a warrant have been issued, you can readily understand why the women ultimately take the law into their own hands or despair of finding relief at all. Or why the male feels protected by the system in his use of violence. (p. 5)

Truninger (1971) surveyed seven legal service offices in San Francisco and Sacramento and 21 attorney members of the Family Law Section of the San Francisco Bar Association to find out their perceptions of the effectiveness of the criminal justice system in handling family violence cases. In response to the question of whether or not the attorneys felt the system was doing it job, she wrote:

Less than one-fourth of the attorneys felt that the police were of help to their clients in dealing with violence. Few of the attorneys in private practice had filed criminal complaints with the district attorney's office. Those who had advised their clients to file charges believed the solution was ineffective. Most legal service attorneys . . . felt that restraining orders were of little value stating that police will refuse to enforce the restraining order . . . or because it will be ignored by the . . . husbands. Restraining orders and orders to vacate the home must be obtained in dissolution proceedings, so they are not responsive to emergency situations. (Truninger, 1971, p. 271)

39

Mental Health Services

The criminal justice system was not the only professional group found ineffective in its response to the needs of battered women. Mental health was also found wanting (Truninger, 1971). One therapist reported the problem was that it usually took five or six sessions before the battered wife would admit she was beaten by her husband. Typically she came into the clinic complaining of depression or difficulty sleeping or some psychosomatic ailment. This therapist went on to point out that the national average for the number of sessions a client attends therapy before dropping out is five or six. In other words, the women drop bout of treatment just abut the time they are ready to disclose they are being beaten.

The attorneys surveyed felt that even if their clients went to therapy little was done for them.

Those private attorneys who had experience with marriage counseling believed that it is generally ineffective. As one attorney put it: counseling is done in a limited time, the problems are handled superficially if they are identified at all, and often the assailant will not participate. (Truninger, 1971, p. 275)

Community Attitudes

Concluding her comments about the results of her survey, Truninger (1971) wrote:

Despite the volume of legislation dealing with marital violence, most attorneys perceived the system as basically ineffective. This is due in large part to the attitude of agencies responsible for carrying out the legal provisions. Namely they are oriented to nonenforcement. (p. 275)

Symonds (1975), in an attempt to understand the reason for the attitude that blames the victim and withholds needed services and community support, wrote:

This response to victims stems from a basic

40

need for all individuals to find a rational explanation for violence, particularly brutal crimes. Exposure to senseless, irrational, brutal behavior makes one feel vulnerable and helpless. It makes one feel that it can happen at any time, in any place to anyone. It is a relief to believe that the victim has done something or neglected something that plausibly contributed to the crime. It makes the other person feel less helpless and less vulnerable. (p. 20)

The word "victim" originally meant a person or animal to be sacrificed in a religious ritual. The victim, like the scapegoat, was used by the community as a purgative to absolve itself of its collective guilt. "The sacrifice of the victim or the exclusion of the scapegoat would symbolically make the rest of the community safe from harm" (Symonds, 1975, p. 21). The community harbors attitudes that prevent sympathetic and empathetic responses for the victim and chief among them is the unconscious fear of contamination by the victim who is believed to be tainted and unclean. "The result of this primitive response of fear is to isolate or exclude the victim" (p. 20).

This chapter has presented an outline of the violent episode's three phases and the response of police, the courts, and mental health to the battered woman's request for help. Those who are best able to judge the effectiveness of the criminal justice system feel it has failed to serve battered women. If the battered wife is to be helped it is important that programs be developed that offer real alternatives to what is presently available. These programs must take into consideration the identified needs of physical safety, group support and understanding, job training, and meaningful employment. These needs and others closely related are addressed in the next chapter.

CHAPTER 5

COMMUNITY PROGRAMS

Two model programs designed to meet the needs of abused women are presented. The programs represent a community psychology approach to the problem of wife abuse. After a brief discussion of the community psychologist's theoretical orientation, the chapter introduces two specific programs: the first is a shelter for battered women and their children, the second offers peer counseling and job referral in cooperation with a federally funded job training and placement service.

Community Psychology Approach to
Wife Abuse

In the past decade and a half community psychology has emerged as a comprehensive framework for viewing human behavior and as a guide for social action. According to the community psychologist, human behavior is shaped by the interaction of the individual in society as he progresses through a series of developmental tasks.

All individuals must progress from infancy through childhood by learning progressively more complicated cognitive, social, and emotional tasks . . . successful learning of an earlier task is important for learning later tasks. Such stages are universal . . . successful completion of one stage is a

42

> prerequisite for passage to the next . . .
> successful accomplishment of each stage (is)
> taken to be environmentally determined. . .
> failure to master developmental tasks should
> not be considered to be the result of
> illness, but rather of failure of social
> systems to provide the necessary resources.
> (Rappaport, 1977, p. 58)

In order to implement constructive change, community psychology integrates the principles of public health with those of psychology for the purpose of improving the quality of life. Moreover, community psychology is not limited to a reparative function but attempts to prevent the development of illness.

Rappaport (1977) has distinguished two fundamental aspects of community psychology. One is scientific analysis: the other is direct application. Furthermore, this application implies political involvement As he states, "if the analysis leads to political action, so must the activities of the community psychologist" (p. 4). In short, establishing programs is a political act.

As shown above, the problems of abused women are not limited to the intrapsychic level. Rather, a comprehensive approach must be utilized which community psychology can offer.

Sarason (1974) stated that the goal of community psychology is "to create the conditions in which people can experience a sense of community" (p. 155). "Community" refers to a feeling of belonging and being included. Because of the conditions of abuse, battered wivea tend to feel alienated and alone. Moreover, it has been suggested that alienation and isolation are integral to the dissolution of community structures (Sarason, 1974; Slater, 1970; Stokols, 1975).

Emotional illness results from the unsuccessful resolution of conflict generated during a crisis. Persons in psychological crisis are identified by the community psychologist as "persons-at-risk." They are the focus of attention because timely intervention with those at-risk can serve to avoid or reduce future emotional dysfunction (Caplan, 1964). "Prevention" may be though of as "changing the local conditions within a community or organization in order to improve positive development of persons or reduce negative reactions to stress" (Kelly, 1977, p. 11).

43

Prevention Strategies

The community psychologist serves the population-at-risk with any of three prevention strategies. These strategies are not mutually exclusive but tend to interact and can be viewed as concentric circles, each with a different focus.

Primary Prevention

The first prevention strategy is primary prevention and it involves keeping people identified as at-risk from becoming psychologically dysfunctional. In the case of the battered wife, a primary strategy might be identifying characteristics of abuse women and violent husbands and counseling young engaged couples about the hazards they face. Other strategies aimed at preventing the incidence of wife abuse might include making known the facts and pervasiveness of the problems to help raise the public's consciousness; educate young couples about how to solve marital problems through improved communication and teaching mental health principles in the public schools.

Secondary Prevention

The next form of prevention is "secondary prevention" and it involves establishing programs that provide early detection, prompt and effective treatment, and manipulation of the conditions that lead to the dysfunction. In this way the length of suffering can be substantially reduced. Treatment often involves a form of time-limited crisis intervention where the focus of treatment is placed upon readapting past successful coping strategies. Old skills are relearned and applied to new stressors.

Tertiary Prevention

The last of the prevention strategies is "tertiary prevention," and it aims at providing rehabilitation to those who have been dysfunctional over a longer period of time. Again, its purpose is to reduce the duration of dysfunction. The longer the battered wife remains in a violent relationship the more difficult it will be for her to free herself from abuse. The cumulative effect of years of abuse has compounded the original

44

problems into long standing emotional difficulties. In this case of shelter programs would be vital for providing an alternative to the violent relationship. The next section will describe the shelter and counseling programs. Specific goals and activities are delineated which meet the various needs of battered women, such as physical safety, emotional support, job training, and social advocacy. Physical safety means freedom from bodily harm and threat of its recurrence. Emotional support refers to a warm and accepting psychological atmosphere created through social interaction with peers and staff. Job training provides skills and confidence for seeking material independence. Social advocacy utilizes role modeling as a way of teaching women how to identify their needs, establish priorities and work on getting their needs met. By watching their advocate interact with representatives from various agencies such as welfare or legal aid, the women see first hand the successful ways of dealing with bureaucratic requirements for getting what they need. In this way social advocacy utilizes role models to educate battered women in preparation for their return to independent living.

The Community Shelter Program

√The first goal of the shelter is to provide a refuge for battered women and their children who are fleeing their homes because of conjugal violence. Within the shelter, a house set anonymously in the community, a supportive therapeutic environment will be established which will help the residents lessen their social isolation and rebuild their self-esteem in keeping with the second goal. Rebuilding self-esteem is accomplished by helping a woman to recognize how aspects of herself have been undervalued or denied expression. In the process of helping her accomplish this task, feelings of isolation and the resulting loneliness are reduced.

After what may have been years of social isolation the woman is likely to have outdated skills and unrealistic expectation regarding her position in the job market. For this third goal the staff will help her reasses and prepare to meet the challenges of reentry. The fourth goal is an extension of the third, focusing more specifically on the interaction between the battered woman and the trained staff. The function

45

of social advocacy is to allow the woman a first-hand opportunity to observe successful female role models helping her get her needs met.

Within the above stated goals, the specific objections of the program are: (a) to establish a telephone hotline, (b) to provide physical shelter, (c) to provide psychological counseling and peer support systems, (d) to assist the children with living and school needs, (e) to offer family counseling, (f) to provide follow-up services, (g) to document the incidence of wife abuse, and (h) to provide community education about wife abuse.

The telephone hotline answers emergency telephone calls from women in distress. The operators are trained to answer questions, make proper referrals, provide information about existing services in the community, and in some cases to do emergency counseling on the telephone. These workers would be volunteers from the community at large, and would be utilized only after they have successfully completed a screening and training program. The hotline has been very effective in community action programs aimed at helping those people in crisis.

Group therapy would be designed to help women discover their power as individuals through interpersonal interaction. The group members would work at helping each other understand what their individual strengths and weaknesses are as well as how to capitalize on them. In this way the individuals learn how to be successful group members and eventually they will form the nucleus of a social network of supportive relationships. The group experience will allow the women an opportunity, some for the first time, to express their feelings and to vent their anger.

The children accompanying their mothers often have special needs when living at the shelter. Their home lives have been disrupted by the conjugal violence and the move to the shelter. The uncertainty and strange surroundings may lead to initial withdrawal followed by destructive acting out of pent up feelings. The children need the opportunity to work through their feelings in supervised play therapy sessions. In addition to their emotional needs their formal education must be continued. The shelter personnel will provide transportation to and from school, see that records are transferred, and help facilitate adjustment to a new school when necessary.

If the wives so request, efforts will be made by the staff to involve the husbands in family counseling aimed at the potential restructuring of the family. Following the role model concept, male counselors may prove effective working with husbands prone to violence.

After leaving the shelter the woman is faced with the transition to a novel or restructured environment. She needs continuing contact with the staff in order to maintain a smooth transition. Ongoing groups of former residents will meet periodically to discuss their problems in living and to serve as a support system (Caplan, 1972).

Failure to adequately document the incidence of abuse had impeded efforts to gain community recognition and resultant financial support. Documenting the actual incidence to abuse will involve work with the police department, the hospitals, and various public and private agencies.

The statistical profile generated through the systematic involvement of agencies with the shelter will be made available and programs will be designed to educate the public about wife abuse. Emphasis will be on public media, law enforcement, and service agencies working directly with the women.

Steps in Treatment

When the battered woman arrives at the shelter she will be assisted in determining her immediate needs, and an advocate will be assigned to help her get her needs satisfied. If she has no financial resources she will be helped in getting welfare and, if appropriate, food stamps. Often abused wives have legal questions about dissolution proceedings, child support, spousal support, prosecution of the husband for assault problems concerning bankruptcy, and immigration. The woman's advocate will help make contact with paralegal assistance from the Legal Aid Society.

When possible the advocate will assist in dealing with medical problems, including helping to set up appointments and to provide transportation to the clinic. If the woman is interested in returning to or beginning school, or finding work, she will be counseled in these areas. The shelter staff will facilitate her involvement in the appropriate programs. Assistance will also be offered in locating long-term housing when possible.

47

Goals and Evaluation

An overall multilevel community action approach (see Figure 3) includes three levels: the organization, the program, and the clinical treatment. The organization is the group of people who, for the purpose of the grant or funding source, and responsible for the program and its implementation but are not responsible for delivery of direct services to the clients. They are not to be confused with the staff who are themselves hired to deliver direct services. The organization may be the board of directors of the abused women's community group.

The program is the theoretical and practical ideas that are combined with a hired staff to service the battered wives. The specific objectives and activities the staff performs with the client population is the clinical aspect of the program.

Each of these is further subdivided into long-range planning goals, short-range objectives, and specific activities. The organizational level involves the entire community and overall prevention strategies. The program goals are specific application of the above concepts. Finally, clinical services meets the needs of individual clients. Evaluation should attempt to determine whether goals and objectives are met, or to what extent they are met.

The long-range planning goals for the organization are: (a) to reduce the incidence of family violence; (b) to verify the type and extent of family violence; (c) to establish fiscal policy that will ensure the independence and stability of the program through future funding; (d) to raise the consciousness of the community about causes, extent, and prevention of conjugal violence; (e) to help community agencies become more effective in delivering services to battered women and their children; (f) to develop a unified policy regarding emergency housing for battered women.

Evaluation of the long-range organizational goals should include: recognition of the fact that when the woman is living at the shelter she cannot be the target of abuse. Therefore, the incidence of wife abuse in the community is lowered to the extent that women utilize the shelter. Other considerations are the following:

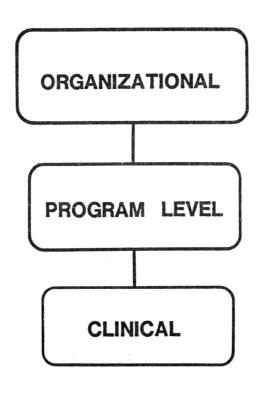

Figure 3.   Hierarchial   structure   in   multilevel community action approach.

1. The director will keep accurate monthly statistics on all clients served, and will provide an end-of-year summary.
2. Fiscal independence will be evaluated based upon the new funding sources located and developed during the year.
3. Accurate records will be kept of all speaking engagements and media contacts along with evaluations from recipients of educational services.
4. Evaluation forms from clients, staff, and referral sources will be utilized to assess the quality of service delivery.

The short-range objectives for the organization are: (a) to break the cycle of family violence by removing the women and their children from the violent home and providing them with shelter; (b) to document the extent and type of abuse experienced by the women; (c) to adopt an accounting system that is consistent with the granter's guidelines for fiscal accountability; (d) to provide community education about the causes, extent, and prevention of conjugal violence; (e) to provide consultation and education to other community agencies on the treatment of battered women; (f) to establish a working committee including the YWCA, the Housing Authority, and other interested parties, to develop a comprehensive emergency housing plan for battered women.

The specific activities of the organization are: (a) to provide emergency transportation, food, clothing, housing, and supportive services at the shelter; (b) to develop intake and statistical forms that will provide for the collection of demographic data, to keep accurate records of each client served, to contact each referral source to ascertain whether client contact had been made and the outcome; (c) to maintain accurate monthly records of expenditures, to develop an ongoing relationship with other funding sources, to maintain an active file of grant and donation sources, and to submit timely grant proposals; (d) to provide speakers for schools, agencies, and citizens' groups; to utilize television, newspapers, and radio to inform the community about conjugal violence and the services the shelter provides; (e) to provide printed material on spouse abuse to agencies, to speak at the agencies on the treatment of battered women and to act as a role model to other professionals delivering services to battered women; (f) to establish a long-term emergency housing committees in which the program director will serve as an active member.

The long-range goals for the program are: (a) to provide a structure, continuity, and organizational flow that will provide effective service delivery to battered women and their dependent children; (b) to establish a workable evaluation format to provide meaningful feedback to the organization for future planning and direction.

The short-range objectives for the program are: (a) to develop policies and procedures that will govern daily operation of the program; (b) to develop appropriate forms and a documentation system.

The specific activities of the program are: (a) to write and, where applicable, to adopt organization personnel policies, including an affirmative action policy; (b) to evaluate the policies that are utilized in order to provide corrective feedback. This will be done in order to maintain consistency between the theoretical base and actual application to battered women.

The long-range clinical service goals are: (a) to help clients function independently, capable of handling their own affairs; (b) to help clients utilize personal and community resources in times of crisis; (c) to remediate the emotional damage done to the children by the violence.

Evaluation of the long-range clinical service goals will: (a) involve utilization of client and staff surveys as well as a log of successfully completed referrals; (b) include completed self-evaluation forms and a daily diary of activities with an emphasis on successfully completed referral contacts. This will demonstrate breaking through the inertia of social isolation and demonstrate a working knowledge of community resources; (c) involve assessment of the change in the children's attitudes and behaviors by their mothers, the counselors, and the children themselves.

The short-range objectives of clinical services are: (a) to help clients recognize their options and choices and to develop a sense of competence; (b) to build clients' self-esteem and reduce their social isolation; (c) to educate the children by role playing new behaviors, and to supply legitimate outlets for pent-up emotions due to conjugal violence.

The specific activities of clinical services are: (a) to facilitate consciousness-raising groups, peer-group counseling, and assertiveness training in order to help the women identify with strong female models; (b) to create a warm, supportive environment, to encourage interaction and participation on the part of all clients, and to introduce the women to available community resources; (c) to provide specific information to the children about the nature of conjugal violence and its potential effects upon them, to provide play therapy and psychodrama to help facilitate the expression of emotions, to provide effective training in parenting skills, to provide outings and activities to help facilitate the children's socialization and break down the emotional barriers resulting from the violence.

These have been specific long-range and short-range goals for a shelter program. There has been no attempt to suggest a precise plan to detailed implementation of these goals. This is because each organization will need to work out its individual strategy when confronting various obstacles in the community. There are numerous strategies for implementation each specific goal, but which remain beyond the scope of the present paper.

The Job Training and Peer Counseling Program

This program is a small scale model for meeting a subset of the objectives as specified in the shelter program. The theoretical cornerstone for this model is derived from research which suggests that women who have jobs are more likely to leave a violent relationship (Gelles, 1976). Several factors serve to explain this phenomenon. First, women who have jobs outside the home are not socially isolated and tend to develop close friendships and support systems. Secondly, women who work have the opportunity to compare living experiences and to recognize alternatives to abuse. Finally, the demands of the job require them to make decisions which enable them to function more independently than their nonworking peers.

The program's objectives are: (a) to involve women in training programs such as Federal Employment Training Commission (FETC) job training; (b) to familiarize women with support and employment services; (c) to organize women into support groups; (d) to

52

coordinate emergency services in the community; (e) to educate the public through media and public information events.

The Federal Employment Training Commission offers career counseling, on-the-job training, and schooling opportunities. This program is designed to act as an administrative arm of FETC to help them achieve success working with battered wives.

Women need to be aware of current employment opportunities, which change rapidly in today's market. New technologies have opened many possibilities for careers and redefinition of old narrow job classifications have made new positions available.

Battered women who have never worked or who have not worked in many years feel inadequate and without support would probably drop out of a job training or schooling program. They need close personal supervision and to belong to a group which gives them support and information.

The program will provide an integration among existing social services and agencies that offer services to battered women. Such coordination can provide the groundwork for future legislation which seeks to prevent or reduce the severity of the problem.

The program will interface with FETC by preparing battered women psychologically to enter the job training programs. It will focus on such issues as utilization of time, budget planning, interpersonal communication skills, and values clarification as well as assertiveness training. Women lacking these skills are not likely to succeed on the job.

Individual counselors will be assigned to each woman who enters the program, and they will follow her progress throughout her stay in her FETC training program. The counselor will do a 6-month follow-up after the woman has either completed her training or dropped out.

These have been two models for programs to assist battered women deal with problems in living. There are many possibilities in how to implement individual goals and objectives. These programs were designed to offer physical safety, supportive peer-group counseling, and job training in order to help beaten women find their personal strength and begin to act independently. Helping these women are a trained staff of successful women acting as role models and social advocates which help train the women and teach them how to fend for themselves.

53

The next chapter summarizes what has appeared in the first five chapters and includes a schematic representation of the interlocking systems affecting conjugal terrorism. The chapter concludes with recommendations for future research and program development from a community psychology perspective.

CHAPTER 6

SUMMARY AND RECOMMENDATIONS

This chapter presents an overview of the first five chapters. Following this is a schematic representation of the interrelationships among the variables affecting conjugal terrorism. The chapter concludes with a look at possible future research and community action projects.

The purpose of this dissertation has been to examine the separate elements affecting wife abuse in an attempt to bring them together in a comprehensive theoretical framework. Having proposed a framework from which to understand the issues involved in conjugal violence, two models for programs were presented that are designed to reduce or eliminate the problems of abuse. These models reflect a community psychology orientation to wife abuse.

The battered wife, in many cases as a result of early trauma, suffers from extremely low self-esteem. In order to compensate for deep feelings of inadequacy she overcompensates by highlighting the culturally valued feminine characteristic of passive acceptance, hoping this will make her worthy. These women often feel compelled to accept their fate no matter how miserable or degraded it makes them feel. In this context, violence is just another burden to bear. These women suffer from what can be termed "neurotic acceptance."

Historically, the cultural roots of wife abuse have resulted in community-wide support for the idea that husbands have a duty, if not a right to beat their wives if only to teach them their proper place in society. The combination of cultural reinforcement for the use of violence, and low self-esteem has kept these women from identifying their problem and seeking help from others in the community.

The violent husband, also as a result of early trauma, has become alienated from his feelings of self-worth and develops a compelling need to overcompensate for deep feelings of inadequacy. As he begins to identify himself with an idealized self-image, he becomes emotionally invested in a false self, and develops "neurotic pride." Once he has established this alliance within himself, he is under great pressure to live up to this inflated image. Suffering from severe self-doubt and lacking self-worth, he experiences even normal challenges as attacks on his right to exist so that he felt compelled to counter-attack with violence to ensure his survival.

Cultural and historical support for their neurotic development keeps the violent husbands alienated from their feelings, hopelessly trapped in an endless search for partial fulfillment. "Having once had legal and religious sanctions to chastise their wife, some men have confused their responsibility and believe they must control and dominate her. Feeling threatened by uncontrollable feelings from within, they believe they must crush any independent functioning in their wives. These men become "conjugal terrorists."

The couple's violent episode has a cyclical pattern which fluctuates as it rises and falls with the building of tension. Much like the cycles of biological arousal, the violent couple feels the tension between them build to an explosion, followed by the husband's desire for closeness and conciliation. The wife, numbed and shocked, regains her senses and is angry, hurt, and feeling betrayed.

During the first few incidences of violence, she is likely to call the police for help. In some cases she may call a friend or relative for support and advice. However, the general attitudes are likely to make her feel guilty and responsible for his violence. Often the "advice" is one of encouragement to stay in the relationship. She may make several attempts to flee, but lack of a job and little, if any, money usually combined with several small children means she is very likely to return to her husband. It is not unusual for her husband to pursue her in an attempt to get her to return to him, all the while threatening her and those who aid her with physical harm if she does not return. After several attempts she surrenders and gives up trying.

The police and courts, when they are called upon, are of little help and may actually contribute to the violence. The police and courts are traditional, male-dominated institutions socialized in very much the same manner as the violent husband. They, like the violent husband, tend to see women as the property of men. Many continue to see women as legal minors rather than fully vested citizens. The result is that women who file court actions are made to feel as if they are criminals.

The court, in a misguided effort to keep the family together at all costs, has stressed conciliation rather than prosecution. This policy has meant that battered wives are forced to return to violent homes. Arresting officers have been known to frighten women contemplating legal action with the idea that prosecuting her husband would lead to financial disaster for her and the children. Some officers have suggested that by pressing charges against her violent husband she is depriving the children of their father.

If it responds at all, the community response to the plight of battered women has been to ignore the problem. Should denial fail, the response is then to blame the victim, intimating that the violence is deserved.

It is the community that holds the key to the treatment of battered wives because it holds the psychological and financial resources that would free the women from their torment. With the establishment of programs designed specifically for battered women, the community does two things:

1. It legitimizes the struggle of battered women for equal protection under the law.
2. It provides physical safety and an opportunity for the woman to free herself from the tyranny of economic dependence.

Figure 4 is a representation of the interlocking systems affecting conjugal terrorism. The diagram depicts the connection between the violent husband and the accepting wife, each supported in his/her role by community attitudes, and the three levels of intervention: (a) legal, (b) psychological, and (c)

57

community.   Each of these intervention levels will   be
discussed briefly in the next section.

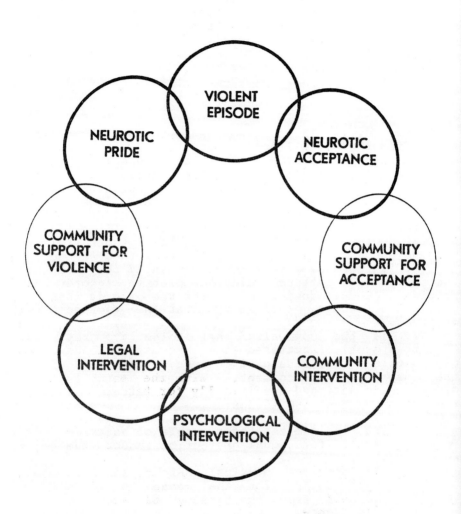

Figure 4.   Representation of interlocking   systems
                      affecting conjugal terrorism

Legal Intervention

There has been a recent change in the California law affecting wife abuse. Previously men who abused their wives were tried for Assault under Section 245a of the California Penal Code. However, because of inadequate enforcement a change in the law was necessary.

Police officers arriving at the scene of conjugal violence had to determine whether a misdemeanor or felony had been committed. The misdemeanor, a less serious charge, must occur in the presence of the arresting officer for him to take legal action, according to the law. In order to help the officer make this determinating a simple, informal rule was used to establish if the crime was severe enough to be considered a felony. Known as the "five stitch rule," it said that, in effect, wounds that required five stitches to close would indicate a felony had been committed.

One solution to this problem would be if the battered wife would institute a citizen's arrest. In this way the police officer need not be present during the commission of the crime in order for him to make the arrest. However, the battered wife usually does not know her rights and the police are generally reluctant to inform her as to what her rights are.

Another solution has been offered with the addition into the California Penal Code of Wife Abuse 273d. This addition means that wife abuse will automatically be a felony. Besides making the officer's job easier, the change has an additional benefit by allowing for the collection of statistical data which had previously been unattainable. Under 245a, the district attorney could prosecute a violent husband but there was no way of recording the assault as wife abuse. As a result it was impossible to document the extent of the problem, ironically, the very information needed by governmental agencies to help determine allocation of funds for community action programs.

Psychological Intervention

Traditionally, treatment for wife abuse has consisted of individual psychotherapy for the wife; the husband almost invariably refused treatment, as he did not accept that he had a problem. While this form of treatment was well meant, it was ineffective. The couple was divided into "good" and "bad" categories and one or the other was punished.

What is needed is a new approach, a systems or community approach. In a systems approach, the problem of violence is not defined as a complete cause and effect relationship between an individual and his behavior, but as a problem in living involving the interplay of the individual and environmental factors. These factors contribute to the creation and maintenance of undesirable behavior.

As part of their orientation, community psychologist look at these factors which potentially reinforce conjugal violence. Once there factors are identified strategies are designed to alter them. In the case of the violent family, the factor that perpetuates the violence is that they continue to live together. If either one leaves the home the violence stops. As the husband does not believe he has a problem and the wife is in imminent danger of physical harm, it is concluded that to provide a refuge for her would be the most efficacious step toward treatment.

Community Intervention

Community intervention involves the design and implementation of specific therapeutic programs aimed at preventing, reducing, or rehabilitating victims of abuse. Two programs have already been proposed in the previous chapter, one which described a shelter providing physical safety of the woman and another program offering job training opportunities as well as peer support groups.

These programs are just the beginning of the attempt to solve the problems of victims of violent crime. Victims of violent crime are displaced from their normal lives and suffer traumatic readjustments as a result of the crime. In the broad context of this group the battered wife is a significant element and must be figured into rehabilitative efforts aimed at victims of violent crime.

Recommendations for Future Research

An important area in need of further investigation

60

involves violent husbands. Presently there are no such investigations taking place. Complicating the matter of research is the fact that violent husbands refuse to identify themselves. These men continue to remain hidden because the community does not challenge their use of violence.

In order to help facilitate further research the community psychologist could begin a self-help group of violent husbands and in this way encourage them to identify themselves. Once identified, more scientifically oriented research could proceed. This research would include data collection, measurement of behavior and attitudes, and development of intervention strategies.

This type of group should be a part of a more comprehensive study effort examining cultural attitudes and behaviors that support violence in the community. Men living in a complex and competitive society are pressured to act in many ways that are potentially destructive to themselves and others. The community needs to look at possible alternatives to stressful lifestyles. It is unrealistic to expect violent husbands to stop acting violently while the rest of the community continues with its unabated use.

Recommendations for Future Action

Community psychologists have an opportunity to impact the areas of victim assistance and delivery of emergency services by planning coordinating strategies as consultants to police departments. Several police departments around the country have become interested in using psychologists to help reduce the stress related to police work. One way to accomplish this would g to reduce the complexity of the police officer's job.

Recent estimates by police from around the country have shown that only about 15% of the police officer's time is spent relating to matters of crime, and that 85% is spent assisting the general public. It is beginning to appear that the traditional role of the police officer is changing. It seems that in many ways the police officer is a community crisis worker in uniform on 24-hour call.

Recognition of this change prompts the suggestion for a community intervention strategy that operates at two levels. The first level involves development of referral resources and the second involves expanded educational opportunities for police officers. The two dovetail so that what information is gathered in developing referral resources is shared with police officers during inservice training seminars.

Police need community support in the form of referral or backup services. When the officer calls upon a referral source he is materially lessening his burden of responsibility and offering a higher level of service. It would be in the police department's best interest to have many backup services available to them in an emergency. At the same time there are many self-help groups working at the grass roots level trying to solve problems in the community. These groups offer expertise, volunteer manpower, interest, and concern about problems that affect the quality of life in the community. If the police department could create a Bureau of Victim Services, whose job it would be to coordinate these grass roots organizations so that professional and volunteer organizations could interface, it would be solving two major problems related to job stress.

By calling upon the community to help assist itself, the police are recognizing that it impossible for them to be all things to all people. At the same time they are willing to utilize those people in the community who by virtue of training and interest have the necessary skills to be effective.

Through the Bureau of Victim Services the police department could help establish a community Victim Advocacy Coalition with representatives from interested public and private agencies as well as individual citizens meeting regularly to plan effective community-wide intervention strategies to help reduce the impact of violent crime in the community. In addition this group could lobby for changes in legislation or propose legislation that could reduce the amount of trauma the victim experiences.

Concluding Remarks

Community psychology is not longer the mere stepchild for scientific investigation. Scientists who have asked themselves how it is possible to coordinate the pursuit of science with the moral values and obligations of community citizenship are finding their answer in community psychology. Community psychology has seized the energy generated from the human rights movement of the late 1960s and early 1970s and is taking it to new levels of community action. Using principles from clinical research, community psychology accepts the challenge and takes mental health concepts into the community for the purpose of improving the total quality of human life.

BIBLIOGRAPHY

Altman, I. The Environment and Social Behavior: Privacy, Personal Personal Space, Territory, Crowding. Monterey, CA: Brooks/Cole, 1975.

Anynymous letter to Human Behavior Magazine. September, 1977.

Ann Arbor News. Ann Arbor, MI. September 18, 1975, Compliant No. 13626.

Aphra, ,972, 3(1), 48.

Ardrey, R. The Territorial Imperative. New York: Atheneum, 1966.

Bakker, C. B., & Bakker-Rabdau, M. K. No Trespassing: Explorations in Human Territoriality. San Francisco: Chandler & Sharp, 1973.

Ball, M. Issues of violence in family casework. Social Casework, January 1977, pp. 3-12.

Bandura, A. Aggression: A Social Learning Analysis. New Jersey: Prentice-Hall, 1973.

Bandura, A., Ross, D., & Ross, S. A. Transmission of Aggression Through Imitation of Aggressive Models. Journal of Abnormal and Social Psychology, 1961, 16, 575-582.

Bannon, J. Law Enforcement Problems With Intra-Family Violence. Paper presented to the American Bar

64

Association Convention, August 12, 1975.

Berliner, B. On Some Psychodynamics of Masochism. Psychoanalytic Quarterly, 1947, 16, 459-471.

Berliner, B. The Role of Object Relations in Moral Masochism. Psychoanalytic Quarterly, 1958, 27, 38-56.

Bettelheim, B. Symbolic Wounds: Puberty Rites and the Envious Male. New York: Collier, 1954.

Bible, English: The Parallel Bible. London: H. Frowde, 1885.

Bordua, D. J. Juvenile Delinquency and "Anomie": An Attempt at Replication. Social Problems, 1958, 6, 230-239.

Brownmiller, S. Against Our Will. New York: Simon & Schuster, 1975.

Calhoun, J. B. Population Density and Social Pathology. Scientific America, 1962. 206, 139-148.

Caplan, G. Principles of Prevention Psychiatry. New York: Basic Books, 1964.

Support Systems. Address to Conference of Department of Psychiatry, Rutgers Medical School and New Jersey Mental Health Association, newark, NJ, June 8, 1972.

Carlson, B. Battered Women and Their Assailants. Social Work, 1977, 455-460.

Cavan, R. S. Suicide. Chicago: University of Chicago Press, 1928.

Chapin, F. S. Some Housing Factors Related to Mental Hygine. Journal of Social Issues, 1951, 7, 164-171.

Christian, J., Flyger, V., & Davis, D. Factors in the Mass Mortality of a Herd of Silka Deer Cervus Nippon. Chesapeake Science, 1960, 1, 79-95.

Coser, L. A. Continuities in the Study of Social

Conflict. New York: The Free Press, 1967.

Dahrendorf, R. Essays in the Theory of Society. Stanford, CA: Stanford University Press, 1968.

Davidson, T. Wifebeating: A Recurring Phenomenon Throughout History. In M. Roy (Ed.), Battered Women: A Psychosociological Study in Domestic Violence. New York: Van Norstand Reinhold, 1977.

Davis, N. A. The Reasons of Misrule: Youth Groups and Charivaris in Sixteenth Century France. Past and Present, 1971.

DeLong, A. J. Territorial Stability and Hierarchial Formation. Small Group Behavior, 1973, 4, 56-63.

Dollard, J., Doob, L., Miller, N. E., Mower, O. H., & Sears, R. Frustration and Aggression. New Haven: Yale University Press, 1939.

Dosey, M. A., & Meisels, N. Personal Space and Self Protection. Journal of Personality and Social Psychology, 1969, 11, 93-97.

Eisenberg, S. E., & Micklow, P. A. The Assaulted Wife: "Catch 22" Revisited (An exploratory legal study of wifebeating in Michigan). Unpublished manuscript, University of Michigan Law School, 1974.

Elbow, M. Theoretical Considerations of Violent Marriages. Social Casework, November 1977, pp. 515-526.

Elliot, F. A. The Neurology of Explosive Rage: The Dyscontrol Syndrome. In M. Roy (Ed.), Battered Women: A Psychosociological Study of Domestic Violence. New York: Van Norstrand Reinhold, 1977.

Esser, A. H. Cottage Fourteen: Dominance and Territoriality in a Group of Institutionalized Boys. Small Group Behavior, 1973, 4, 131-146.

Faris, R., & Dunham, H. W. Mental Disorders in Urban Areas. Chicago: Phoenix Books, 1965.

Faulk, M. Men Who Assault Their Wives. Medicine,

Science and the Law, 1974, 14, 180-183.

Flynn, J. P. Recent Findings Related to Wife Abuse. Social Casework, January 1977, pp. 13-20.

Foreman, T., & Templeton, B. Sporting Life. The Fresno Bee, March 10, 1978, D-5.

Franklin, S. S., & Mitchell, R. P The Effect of Crowding on Social Organization in Children. Unpublished manuscript, 1973.

Freud, A. The Ego and the Mechanism of Defense. New York: International Universities Press, 1966.

Galle, O. R., Grove, W. R., & McPherson, J. M. Population Density and Pathology: What are the Relations for Man. Science, 1972, 176, 23-30.

Garver, N. What Violence Is. The Nation, June 24, 1968, pp. 1-13.

Gayford, J. J. Wife Battering: A Preliminary Survey of 100 Cases. British Medical Journal, 1975, 25, 194-197.

Battered Wives One Hundred Years Ago. The Practitioner, 1977, 122-128. (a)

The Plight of the Battered Wife. International Journal of Environmental Studies, 1977, 10, 183-286. (b)

Gelles, R. J. Child Abuse as Psychopathology: A Sociological Critique and Reformulation. Americal Journal of Orthopsychiatry, 1973, 43 611-621.

The Violent Home. Beverly Hills, CA: Sage Publications, 1974.

The Social Construction of Child Abuse. American Journal of Orthopsychiatry, 1975. 45, 363-371.

Abused Wives: Why Do They Stay? Journal of Marriage and the Family, 1976, 38(10), 659-668.

Gelles, R., & Straus, M. Determinants of Violence in the Family: Toward a Theoretical Integration. In

W. Burr, R. Hill, F. Nye, & I. Reiss (Eds.), Contemporary Theories About the Family. New York: The Free Press, 1978.

Gil, D. G. Violence Against Children. Journal of Marriage and the Family, 1971, 33, 637-648.

Unraveling Child Abuse. American Journal of Orthopsychiatry, 1975, 45,346-355.

Goldstein, J. H. Aggression and Crimes of Violence. New York: Oxford University Press, 1975.

Goldstein, S. Separation-Individuation: Relationship to Normal Growth and Development and Psychopathology. Unpublished doctoral dissertation, California School so Professional Psychology, Fresno, 1977.

Goode, W. J. Force and Violence in the Family. Hournal of Marriage and the Family, 1971, 33, 624-636.

Gray, J. The Psychology of Fear and Stress. New York: World University Library, McGraw-Hill, 1971.

Gurr, T. R. Why Men Rebel. Princeton: Princeton University Press, 1970.

Hall, E. T. The Hidden Dimension. New York: Doubleday, 1966.

Harlow, H. F. Learning to Love. new york: Jason ARonson, 1974.

Hays, H. R. The Dangerous Sex: The Myth of Feminine Evil. New York: G. P. Putnam's Sons, 1964.

Hobbes, T. Hobbes' Leviathan. Oxford: The Clarendon Press, 1909.

Homans, G. Fundamental Social Processes. In N. Smelser (Ed.), Sociology. New York: Wiley, 1967.

Horney, K. Neurosis and Human Growth: The Struggle Toward Self-Realization. New York: norton, 1950.

Hornstein, H. A. Cruelty and kindness: A New Look at Aggression and Altruism. Englewoon Cliffs, NJ: Prentice-Hall, 1976.

Hymans, E. Terrorists and Terrorism. New York: St. Martin Press. 1974.

Jacobs, P., Brunton, M., & Melville, M. Agressive Behavior, Mental Subnormality and the XYY Male. Nature, 1965, 208, 1351-1352.

Jacobsen, T. Mesopotamia, In H. & H. A. Frankfort, J. Wilsonn, T. Jacobsen, & W. Irwin (Eds.), The Intellectual Adventure of Ancient Man. Chicago: The University of Chicago Press, 1946.

Jackson, S. In Search of Equal Protection for Battered Wives. Unpublished monograph, 1975.

Jenkins, B. Internationa Terrorism: A New Mode of Conflict. Los Angeles: California Seminar on Arms Control and Foreign Policy, Crescent Publications, 1975.

Jourard, S. M. Some Psychological Aspects of Privacy. Law and Contemporary Problems, 1966, 31, 307-318.

Kardener, S. H., & Fuller, M. Violence as a Defense Against Intimacy. Mental Hygiene, 1970, 54, 310-315.

Kelly, J. G. The Search for Ideas and Deeds That Work. In G. W. Albee and J. M. Jaffe (Eds.), Primary Prevention of Psychopathology (Vol. 1.). Hanover, NH: University Press of New England, 1977.

Kempe, C. H. et al. The Battered Child Syndrome. Journal of the American Medical Association, 1962, 181, 17-24.

King, C. H. The Ego and the Integrationof Violence in Homocidal Youth. American Journal of Orthophychiatry, 1975, 45(1), 134-145.

Kinzel, A. S. Body Buffer Zone in Violent Prisoners. American Journal of Psychiatry, 1970, 127, 59-64.

Kira, A. The Bathroom. Ithica NY: Cornell University Center for Housing and Environmental Studies, 1966.

Klein, M. The Psychoanalysis of Children. New York: Delecorte Press/Seymour Lawrence, 1975.

Lander, B. Toward an Understanding of Juvenile Delinquency. New York: Columbia University Press, 1954.

Langley, L. L. Homeostasis. New York: Van Nostrand Reinhold, 1965.

Langley, R., & Levy, R. C. Wife Beating: The Silent Crisis. New York: E. P. Dutton, 1977.

Lantz, H. R. Population Density and Psychiatric Diagnosis. Sociology and Social Research, 1953, 37, 322-326.

Leakey, R. E., & Lewin, R. Is It Our Culture, Not Our Genes, That Makes us Killers? Smithsonian, 1977, 8(8), 56-65.

Lederer, W. The Fear of Women. New York: Harcourt, Brace, Jovanovich, 1968.

Lerner, M. J., & Simmons, C. H. Observers' Reactions to the "Innocent Victim": Compassion or Rejection? Journal of Personality and Social Psychology, 1966, 4, 203-210.

Levin, J. The Functions of Prejudice. New York: Harper & Row, 1975.

Levine M. B. Interpersonal Violence and Its Effects On the Children: A Study of 50 Families in General Practice. Medicine, Science and the Law, 1975, 15(31), 36-48.

Levinger, G. Sources of Marital Dissatisfaction Among Applicants for Divorce. American Journal of Orthopsychiatry, 1966, 36, 803-807.

Leyhausen, P. Dominance and Territoriality as Complimented in Mammalian Social Structure. In A. H. Esser (Ed.), Behavior and Environment: The Use of Space by Animals and Men. New York: Plenum, 1971.

Lorenz, K. On Aggression. New York: Harcourt, Brace,

Jovanovich, 1966.

Lottier, S. Distribution of Criminal Offenses in Metropolitan Regions. Journal of Criminal Law and Criminology, 1938, 29, 39-45.

Lyman, S. M., & Scott, M. B. Territoriality: A Neglected Sociological Dimension. Social Problems, 1967, 15, 235-249.

Lystad, M. H. Violence at Home: A Review of Literature. American Journal of Orthopsychiatry, 1975, 45(3), 328-345.

Malinowski, B. Sex And Repression in Savage Society. Cleveland, OH: The World Publishing Company, 1927.

Martin, D. Battered Wives. San Francisco: Glide Publications, 1976.

Maslow, A. Toward A Psychology of Being. New York: Van Norstrand, 1962.

May, R. Power and Innocence: A Search for the Sources of Violence. New York: W. W. Norton, 1972.

Mill, J. S. The Subjugation of Women. Cambridge, MA: M.I.T. Press, 1970.

Owens, D. M., & Straus, M. A. The Social Structure of Violence in Childhood and Approval of Violence as an Adult. Aggressive Behavior, 1975, 1, 193-211.

Parry, A. Terrorism From Robespierre to Arafat. New York: The Vanguard Press, 1976.

Prescott, S., & Letko, C. Battered Women: A Social Psycholigical Perspective. In M. Roy (Ed.), Battered Women: A Psychosociological Study of Domestic Violence. New York: Van Norstrand Reinhold, 1977.

Queen, S. A. The Ecological Study of Mental Disorders. American Sociological Review, 1948, 5, 201-209.

Rappaport, J. Community Psychology. New York: Holt, Rinehart, & Winston, 1977.

Rappaport, J., & Chinsky, J. M. Models for Delivery of Services from a Historical and Conceptual Perspective. Professional Psychology, 1974, 5, 42-50.

Roy, M. (Ed.) Battered Women: A Psychosociological Study of Domestic Violence. New York: Van Norstrand Reinhold, 1977.

Ruotolo, A. K. Neurotic Pride and Homocide. The American Journal of Psychoanalysis, 1975, 35, 1-16.

Ryan, W. Blaming the Victim. New York: Random House, 1971.

Sainsbury, P. Suicide in London. New York: Basic Books, 1956.

Sarason, S. B. The Psychological Sense of Community: Prospectives for a Community Psychology. San Francisco: Jossey-Bass, 1974.

Schmid, C. Suicide in Minneapolis, Minnesota 1928.1932. American Journal of Sociology, 1933, 39, 30-49.

Schmitt, R. C. Density, Delinquency and Crime in Honolulu. Sociology and Social Research, 1957, 41, 274-276.

Schreiber, J. The Ultimate Weapon--Terrorists and World Order. New York: Willian Morrow, 1978.

Seligman, M. P. Learned Helplessness and depression in Animals and Men. Morristown, NY: General Learning Press, 1976.

Shainess, N. Psychological Aspects of Wifebeating. In M. Roy (Ed.), Battered Women: A Psychosociological Study of Domestic Violence. New York: Van Norstrand Reinhold, 1977.

Singer, J. L. (Ed.) The Control of Aggression and Violence. New York: Academic Press, 1971.

Slater, P. The Pursuit of Loneliness: Americal Culture at the Breaking Point. Boston: Beacon Press,

1970.

Smirnoff, V. N. The Masochistic Crontract. _Inter-national Psychoanalysis,_ 1969, 50 665-671.

Snell, J. E., Rosenwald, R. J., & Robey, A. The Wife Beater's Wife: A Study of Family Interaction. _Archives of General Psychiatry,_ 1964, 2, 107-112.

Spenser, H. _Man vs. the State._ Caldwell, ID: The CastonPrinters, 1940.

Spiegel, R. Anger and Acting Out: Masks of Depression. _American Journal of Psychotherpay,_ 1967, 2, 597-600.

Star, B. _Psychosocial Aspects of Wife Battering._ Paper presented at California Attorney General's Conference on Domestic Violence, Los Angeles, A ril 1978.

Star, B., Clark, C., Goetz, K., & O'Malia, L. Comparing Battered and Non-Battered Woman. _Victimology,_ 1978, 3, 32-44.

Steele, B. F., & Pollock, C. B. A Psychiatric Study of Parents Who Abuse Infants and Small Children. In R. E. Helfer & C. H. Kempe (Eds.), _The Battered Child._ Chicago: University of Chicago Pres, 1974.

Steinmetz, S., & Straus, M. A. (Eds.) _Violence in the Family._ New York: Harper & Row, 1974.

Stokols, D. Toward a Psychological Theory of Alenation. _Psychological Review,_ 1975, 82, 26-44.

Straus, M. A. Leveling, Cevility, and Violence in the Family. _Journal of Marriage and the Family,_ 1974, 36, 13-29.

Straus, M. A. Sexual Inequality, Cultural Norms, and Wife-Beating. In E. C. Viano (Ed.), _Victim and Society._ Washington, D.C.: Vintage Press, 1976.

Straus, M. A., Gelles, R. J., & Steinmetz, S. K. _Violence in the Family: An Assesment of Knowledge and Research Needs._ Unpublished manuscript, 1976.

Symonds, M. Victims of Violence: Psychological Effects and After Effects. The Americal Journal of Psychoanalysis, 1975, 35 19-26.

Thornton, T. P. Terror as a Weapon of Political Agitation. In H. Eckstein (ed.), Internal War. New York: Free Press, 1964.

Truninger, E. Marital Violence: The Legal Solutions. Hastings Law Journal, 1971, 23, 259-271.

Valins, S., & Baum., A. Residential Group Size, Social Interaction and Crowding. Environment and Behavior, 1973, 5, 421-440.

Walker, L. Battered Woman. New York: Harper & Row, 1979.

Walster, E., Berscheid, E., & Walster, G. W. New Directions in Equity Research. Journal of Personality and Social Psychology, 1973, 25(2), 151-176.

Warrior, B. Wifebeating. Houseworker's Handbook. Cambridge, MA:

Waston, F. M. Political Terrorism: The Threat and the Purpose. Washington, D.C.: Robert B. Luce, 1976.

Wedge, R. F. A Review of the Literature on the Antecedents of Adolescent Aggression and Delinquency. California Youth Authority, 1977.

Wilkinson, P. Political Terrorism. Londonn: The Macmillian Press, 1974.

Wolfgang, M. E. Husband-Wife Homicides. Corrective Psychiatry and Journal of Social Therapy, 1956, 2, 263-271.

Wolfgang, M., & Ferracuti, F. The Subculture of Violence. New York: Barnes & Noble, 1967.

Yachnes, E. Neurotic Pride. The American Journal of Psychoanalysis, 1975, 35, 27-32.

74

APPENDICES

APPENDIX A

COMMUNITY SHELTER PROGRAM FOR ABUSED WIVES

Anticipated Funding Sources

(Name of Source and Amount Requested)

X	City		$ 36,375.55
X	County		19,586.84
	United Way		
		Sub Total	55,962.39
X	CETA (include title and number of positions)		
	Eight (8) positions - Night Time		38,263.61
	Supervisors		
		Sub Total	38,261.81
X	State		30,250.00
		Sub Total	30,250.00
	Federal		
		Sub Total	
	Other (Donation, Fund Raising, Fees, Etc.)		
		Sub Total	
	GRAND TOTAL OF ABOVE AMOUNTS		$ 124,476.00

II. **PROJECT FUNDING:** (Explain why organization is requesting funding from either the City/County and/or the United Way.)

Our organization is requesting S.B. 91 money which is earmarked as "seed" money to fund a shelter. This money will not cover the entire cost of the shelter. Therefore, in order to demonstrate local community support, we are asking the City-County Revenue Sharing to fund the difference between State money, CETA funds, and the cost of the program.

III. **PROJECT/SERVICE/DESCRIPTION:** (Briefly describe the purpose of this project/service.)

The purpose of this project is to provide a safe refuge to women and children who must flee their home due to spousal violence. Within this shelter a supportive, therapeutic environment will enable the residents to lessen social isolation and rebuild self-esteem. The shelter will also provide positive role models through interaction with the staff. The shelter will also serve as a focal point for community services dealing with family violence.

IV. **COMMUNITY NEED AND/OR PROBLEM:** (Describe in detail how the County area(s) and need(s) or problem(s) to be addressed by the project/service was identified.)

Wife beating is a national epidemic. Recent statistics indicate as many as 50% of American wives are abused. One study shows 20% of middle class divorces and 40% of working class suffer physical abuse. In 1974, 25% of all murders in San Francisco involved legally married or cohabitating mates. FBI statistics indicate that wife battery occurs once every 30 seconds, resulting in 33% of all female homicides. In 1971, 33% of all female homicide victims in California were murdered by their husbands.

Organizations dealing with the problem of spouse abuse are receiving calls at a rapidly increasing rate from battered women seeking shelter. The following statistics indicate the tremendous need

for appropriate shelter: HET is receiving 7-8
calls per week from battered women needing
shelter; the Evangel Home has 4-6 women per month
using their services directly because of
beatings; the YWCA has 3-4 battered women per
month using their facilities: and NOW has 8 calls
per month from women seeking shelter from spouse
abuse.

At present there is no shelter for battered women
and their children escaping violence in the
County. There are minimal emergency housing
services available at the following places. They
all have significant drawbacks. The YWCA accepts
single women only for a fee; the Rescue Mission
accepts only married couples; the Evangel Home
takes no male children over the age of 8 and
requires religious participation; NOW has only 1
emergency room available, fee is involved, and
takes no male children.

It is also important to note that none of the
above facilities offer a supportive or
therapeutic environment geared toward battered
women and their children. These facilities do
not provide any advocacy for their temporary
residents in the way of legal, social, or medical
assistance. These organizations do not keep
statistics on spousal violence, nor do they
coordinate community resources to serve this
needy population.

In our shelter we propose to provide:

1. Emergency housing and food.
2. Advocacy services -- legal, medical, and
   social.
3. Documentation of the problem of spouse abuse
   for future research.
4. Community coordination of resources for
   battered spouses.

V.   TARGET POPULATION:

     A. Show specific breakout of intended consumers
        of services to be offered by this project.
        In each box show a specific breakout by age,
        sex, and ethnicity. In addition, if you use

78

an income standard to establish eligibility
for services, <u>attach</u> the criteria used.

	Child 0-12 years		Youth 13-17 years		Adult 18-59 years		Aged 60+ years Family
Age	300		36		120		
Sex	Male Female	150 150	Male Female	18 18	Male Female	0 120	
Ethnicity	Cauca- sian Mex.Am. Other	120 120 60	Cauca- sian Mex.Am. Other	14 14 8	Cauca- sian Mex.Am. Other	48 48 24	
Sub Totals	300		36		120		

Grand Total: 456

B. Specific geographical areas to be served (for
urban area see attached map), state the
percentage of the total number of eligible
clients to be served within each geographical
area.

VI. **SERVICES:**

A. **LONG-RANGE PLANNING GOALS** of overall program.
(List general organizational or agency
goals.)

<u>Organization Direction Goals</u>
1. To reduce the incidence of family
violence.
2. To validate the type and extent of
family violence.
3. To establish a fiscal policy that will
ensure independence and stability
through future funding.
4. Raise the consciousness of the community
against the causes, extent, and
prevention of family violence.
5. Community agencies will become more
effective in delivering services to
battered women and their children.

6. Unified emergency housing policy and programs.

Program Direction Goals
1. To have a structure, continuity, and organizational flow that will provide effective service delivery to battered women and their children.
2. To establish a workable evaluation format to provide meaningful feedback to the organization for future planning and direction.

Clinical Service Goals
1. Clients will function independently and be capable of handling their own affairs.
2. The individual will have the ability to mobilize and utilize personal and community resources in time of crisis.
3. To remediate the emotional damage done to children due to family violence.

B. **SHORT-RANGE OBJECTIVES** to be achieved during the contract period.

Organization Direction Goals
1. To break the cycle of family violence, we will remove women and children from the violent home and provide them with shelter.
2. To document monthly the extent and type of family violence as displayed by the shelter clients.
3. To adopt an accounting system that's consistent with the granter's guidelines for fiscal accountability.
4. To provide community education about the causes, extent, and prevention of family violence.
5. To provide consultation and education to other community agencies on the treatment of battered women.
6. To establish a working committee compromised of members of the YWCA, Housing Authority, and other interested agencies.

Program Direction Goals
1. To develop policies and procedures that will govern daily operation of the program.
2. To develop appropriate forms and a documentation system.

Clinical Service Goals.
1. To help clients to recognize their options and choices and to develop a sense of competence.
2. To build clients' self-esteem and reduce social isolation.
3. To educate the children by role models to new behaviors; to supply legitimate outlets for pent-up emotions due to family violence.

C. SPECIFIC ACTIVITIES related to accomplishing the short-range objectives.

Organization Direction Goals
1. To provide emergency transportation, food, supportive services to shelter, and clothing.
2. To develop intake and statistical forms that will provide for demographic data to be collected; to keep accurate and specific records on each client served; to contact by phone, person, or letter our referral sources to ascertain whether contact was made and outcome.
3. To maintain accurate monthly expenditure records; to develop an on-going relationship with other funding sources; to maintain an active file on grant and donation sources, and when money is available, to submit grant proposals.
4. To provide speaking engagements for schools, agencies, and citizens' groups; to utilize media--TV, newspaper, and radio--to inform the community about family violence and the services of the shelter.
5. To provide printed material on spouse abuse to agencies, speak at the agencies on the treatment of battered women, and act as a role model to other

professionals delivering services to battered women.

6. The Director of this program will work actively as a member of the emergency housing committee.

Program Direction Goals

1. To write and, where applicable, to adopt organizational and personnel policies, including an affirmative action policy; to evaluate the policies that are utilized in order to provide corrective feedback should changes be necessary. This will be done in order to maintain consistency between our theoretical base and actual application to battered women.

2. To keep accurate, demographic statistics on each client; to keep staff time logs; to utilize client, staff, and referral evaluations to document the appropriateness of our service.

Clinical Service Goals

1. To facilitate consciousness-raising groups; peer-group counseling will be provided; along with assertiveness training; to provide strong, female role models for our clients.

2. To create a warm, supportive environment, to encourage interaction and participation on the part of all clients in the shelter program; to introduce clients directly to available community resources.

3. To provide specific information to children about the nature and effects of family violence upon them; to provide play therapy and psychodrama for appropriate expressions and emotions; to have the staff involved in re-parenting with the mothers of these children; to provide outings and activities to get the children involved with each other to lessen their own isolation.

Program Goals

Through the recent efforts of several women's

groups in exploring the problem of battered
women in the area, it was found that women
involved in physically dangerous and
emotionally damaging situations need a refuge
where they could sort their thoughts, vent
their feelings and frustrations, and have
support in changing the course of their (and
their children's) lives.

We plan to provide support and offer to the
high-risk group of battered women and their
children in the County the following
services: emergency crisis counseling, long-
term counseling, a shelter or refuge,
referrals, and legal information. Also, by
gathering statistics from related agencies
(hospitals, law enforcement groups, mental
health facilities, etc.), we will establish a
documentation center to record the problems
and share this information with the
community. In addition, we will provide or
make available, family couseling to include
the male partners of battered and abused
women.

Program Objectives
1. To offer support, emergency crisis
   counseling, and referrals to battered
   women through a hotline staffed by
   trained volunteers.
2. To offer a weekly self-help support
   group which provides opportunities for
   women to discuss and share their common
   situations and problems.
3. To educate and inform the public, media,
   police, courts, social services, and
   other authorities about battered and
   abused women.
4. To provide temporary shelter or refuge
   for women subjected to family violence
   and their children on request.
   a. If possible, the following options
      will be explored: relatives or
      friends with whom they can stay,
      any other emergency housing
      facilities, or money to pay for a
      hotel.
   b. Only when these possibilities are

exhausted, and the woman is in immediate danger on recurrent, severe beatings will shelter be offered.

c. An advocate will be assigned to ascertain the woman's needs and help get them met; generally, these needs include the following:

1. **Welfare** -- if the battered woman has no possible financial relief or resources, and welfare is her only option, the advocate will help her deal with the Welfare Department.

2. **Legal** -- we anticipate battered women will have legal needs ranging from initiation of dissolution proceedings, child support, and spousal support, to prosecution for felony or misdemeanor wife beating, to bankruptcy and immigration problems. Our legal workers (under the supervision of outside attorneys) will help deal with the legal needs for each woman and accompany her through the legal process. (It has been found by other groups working with battered women that legal advocacy in this area is vitally necessary.)

3. **Medical** -- we will establish procedures at local hospitals to provide medical care for our clients, and we will supply medical advocacy whenever possible.

4. **Vocational Counseling** -- if a woman is interested in returning to or beginning school, or finding work, we will provide her counseling in these areas and help her integrate into appropriate programs.

5. **Relocation Housing** -- besides money, it has been found that the most urgent need of battered women is to find a place to live. Our staff and volunteers will locate low-income and federally supported housing throughout the area and, whenever possible, help the women investigate it.

5. To recognize and care for the emotional and educational need of any children involved.

6. To offer support and aftercare to any women and children who have left the shelter.

7. To provide family counseling to both male and female partners should they wish to participate.

8. To collect data from the police, hospitals, etc., regarding domestic violence and battered women, and to share this information when tabulated.

Program Description

Battered and abused women who feel they have the nonjudgmental support of others, especially women, would be more comfortable in admitting their plight and asking for help. By offering shelter to victims of domestic violence, we would interrupt the vicious cycle of abuse breeding abuse. Also, whether or not children of battered women are themselves beaten, the experience of living within this violence is shattering. Besides being generally destructive psychologically, it prepares them to expect this kind of adult relationship. Interrupting this violence in the next generation is vital.

Numerous police statistics indicate that between 50-85% of family homicides the police had been called at least once. By providing battered women with various avenues of escape or options heretofore unavailable, we would be literally saving lives.

85

Program Strategy

Through numerous newspaper articles, TV and radio appearances, community speaking engagements, etc., many people have indicated a desire to participate in our organization, and we have commitments from the following individuals and agencies: former battered women, private attorneys, social work and psychology students, N.O.W., Department of Public Welfare, Rape Counseling Service, Department of Health, YWCA, Junior Women, Junior League, and Family Service Center.

Our services will be offered to the entire County with emphasis on reaching minority communities. It is universally believed that these communities have very strong family ties and values, very traditional role expectations for men and women, and often a general insulation from other communities.

Periodic orientation sessions will be held to acquaint interested persons with the problem of battered and abused women and their children in our community. Those seriously desiring to volunteer will attend crisis intervention sessions conducted by qualified and empathetic personnel regarding the dynamics of the battered woman and effective crisis intervention techniques. Each volunteer will also explore her/his own experiences with and feelings about violence and victimization.

Legal workers (law students we will recruit from local schools) will be trained by a supervising attorney in the specifics of family law as it relates to the situations of battered women.

What evaluation method and procedures will be utilized in evaluating the above articles?

D. **EVALUATION OF LONG-RANGE GOALS: Organization Direction Goals**
   1. This goal will be evaluated by assessing the total number of people served by the shelter. We base this assessment on the

86

fact that if they are in the shelter, they are not being battered, thereby reducing the incidence of family violence. Statistics and client outcome results will be accumulated, and evaluated.

2. The Director will keep accurate monthly statistics on all clients served, and an end-of-the-year summary will be provided.

3. We will evaluate our fiscal independence by the number of new funding sources that we were able to generate during the year.

4. We will keep accurate records of all speaking engagements and media contacts along with evaluations from recipients of educational services.

5. Evaluation forms from clients, staff, and referral sources will be utilized to assess the quality of service delivery to battered women.

EVALUATION OF LONG-RANGE GOALS: Program Direction Goals

1. The effectiveness of our service delivery will be evaluated by the feedback we receive from our clients and from our referral sources. This feedback will be in writing.

2. We will have available specific evaluation forms that will be utilized by our clients, staff, and referral sources.

EVALUATION OF LONG-RANGE GOALS: Clinical Service Goals

1. We will utilize client and staff evaluations. We will also keep a log of successfully completed referrals.

2. Client will do self-evaluation. A log will be kept of successfully completed referrals to demonstrate that the client has broken through the intertia of social isolation and been able to utilize community resources.

3. Assessment of emotional change in the

children will be made by mothers and the staff.

VII. <u>JOB SPECIFICATIONS AND STAFF TIME USE</u>: (Attach the job specifications for each position shown. Show specifically how each staff person's time is to be spent on each activity to be completed during the one-year funding period.)

A. <u>VOLUNTEERS</u>: If volunteers are to be used in the project/service, state the number to be used and describe the functions and services performed.
1. Three student interns will provide direct clinical services to both adults and children
2. Four volunteer drivers will be used to transport clients and children.
3. Four volunteers will be utilized to help plan and implement children's activities.
4. Two volunteers will be used for field trips and outings for children.

B. <u>JOB SPECIFICATIONS</u>:
1. <u>Coordinator/Counselor</u>: Licensed clinical psychologist--clinical experience with children, or LCSW, clinical experience with children. (Full-time)

Administration: Overall direction and coordination of the agency operation; supervision of clinical interns; fiscal management and development; public relations and program development; liaison to the Board of Directors; responsible for development of operational procedures and overseeing evaluation of project.

Clinical: Responsible for delivery and coordination of clinical services to clients.

2. <u>Assistant Coordinator</u>: Extensive experience with children. (Full-time)

Administration: Supervision of

88

volunteers; assist Director in overall
management of project; act as advocate
for residential clients; supervision and
coordination of night staff; responsible
for transportation of clients during the
day.

Clinical: Work in children's programs.

3. Secretary/Office Manager: General office
management skills and secretarial
skills. (Full-time)

Administration: Type, File, and keep
records.

Clinical: Answer phones.

4. Maintenance Person: Responsible for
maintenance of physical plant. (Half-
time)

5. Night Supervisors: Maintain responsibility for the center during the evening
hours. (70% time)

Administration: Fill out forms and
evaluate clients.

Clinical: Provide emergency coverage
during the night for new clients.

C. STAFF TIME UTILIZATION:
Organizational Direction Goals

Coordinator/Counselor:	40%
Assistant Coordinator:	20%
Secretary:	40%
Maintenance:	0%
Night Supervisors:	20%

Program Direction Goals

Coordinator/Counselor:	30%
Assistant Coordinator:	20%
Secretary:	40%
Maintenance:	100%
Night Supervisors:	20%

VIII. PROPOSED BUDGET -- 1978-1979:

Show Proposed Budget of Organization by Category.

Budget Summary

Line	Budget Categories	Acct. #	Column A
	SALARIES & BENEFITS		
1	Personnel salaries	0100	$ 74,256
2	Employee benefits	0150	10,510
3	Subtotal		84,766
	SERVICES & SUPPLIES		
4	Insurance	0200	5,400
5	Communications	0250	1,800
6	Consultant services	0300	1,600
7	Office expense	0350	1,710
8	Office rental	0400	1,200
9	Equipment rental	0450	400
10	Utilities	0500	2,400
11	Travel (Administration)	0550	400
12	Food Supplies	0600	6,000
13	Contracts	0650	5,000
14	Transportation gas	0700	1,200
15	Van lease	0750	3,600
16	House Rental	0800	9,000
17		0850	
18	Subtotal		39,710
19	TOTAL		$ 124,476

IX. BUDGET DETAIL:

Account Number	Category Description	Subtotal	Total
0100	1. Salaries	$74,256	$74,256
0150	2. Employee benefits	10,510	10,510
0200	3. Insurance: Bonding, liability, fire & theft, auto, general	5,400	5,400
0250	5. Communications: telephone	1,800	1,800
0300	6. Consultant	1,600	4,600
0350	7. Office expense:		
	Typewriter	150	
	Adding Machine	50	
	Furniture	300	
	Stamps	250	
	Consumables	360	1,710
0400	8. Office rental:		
	Building Maintenance	1,200	1,200
0450	9. Equipment rental:		
	Desktop copier	400	400
0500	10. Utilities:		
	Water, sewage, garbage	360	
	Gas	640	
	Electric	1,400	2,400
0550	11. Travel (administration)	400	400
0600	12. Food supplies	6,000	6,000
0650	13. Contracts:		
	Crisis Hotline-HET	3,000	
	Emergency Housing-YWCA	2,000	5,000
0700	14. Transportation - gas	1,200	1,200
0750	15. Van lease	3,600	3,600
0800	16. House rental	9,000	9,000

X.   BUDGET NARRATIVE:

Begin below, and use as many additional pages as necessary, to relate the items budgeted to project activities and complete the required justification of the project budget.

0200   4. Insurance: Figures were arrived at by calling independent insurance agents. Insurance is necessary in order to provide protection to clients and project staff.

0250   5. Telephone: Figure was arrived at by calling the phone company. The telephone is necessary for the staff and clients to conduct normal business, secure community resources, and make referrals.

0300   6. Consultant: Figure was arrived at by asking other agencies. The consultant is necessary to provide legal and financial expertise to ensure proper organizational functioning.

0350   7. Office expenses: Figures were arrived at by calling suppliers. This money is necessary to provide equipment to maintain the proper functioning of the office which allows for continuity of care, keeping of accurate records, and budget management.

0400   8. Office rental: This figure was arrived at by asking other agencies. This money is used to maintain the physical plant, replacing broken or damaged parts.

0450   9. Equipment rental: This figure was arrived at by calling suppliers. The money is necessary to provide for dissemination of written information to keep the staff, public, and agencies aware of program developments.

0500   10. Utilities: This figure was arrived at by calling the utility companies.

Utilities are needed to maintain the physical operation.

0550 11. **Travel (Administration):** This figure was arrived at by asking other agencies. This money is to be spent to help keep the coordinator up to date on other programs throughout the state.

0600 12. **Food supplies:** This figure was arrived at by checking with other agencies. This money will be spent to provide emergency food, available to newly arrived families without food stamps or money.

0650 13. **Contracts:** This figure was arrived at by calling other agencies. Money will be used to pay the YWCA for emergency beds for battered women without children to supplement our program of emergency beds for women with children. Help in Emotional Trouble (HET) will provide emergency hotline and telephone counseling for battered women.

0700 14. **Transportation:** This figure was arrived at by checking with other agencies. This money will be spent for gas which is necessary to provide transportation for women and children to needed services including continued schooling.

0750 15. **Van lease:** This figure was arrived at by calling suppliers. The van is necessary to transport women and children to needed services and continued schooling.

0800 16. **House rental:** This figure was arrived at by calling realtors. The house is necessary to provide emergency shelter to women with children.

APPENDIX B

THE PEER COUNSELING AND JOB TRAINING PROGRAM

Project #VI-095

Applicant:_____

Name of Project:_____

Geographic Jurisdiction:_____

Original Request:$81,575.00 Positions Requested: 8

Amount Negotiated:$67,507.00   %Admin. Cost 15%

Number to be hired: 8   Starting date: 1/3/78

Ending date: 9/28/78

PROJECT DESCRIPTION: Purpose of Project and brief description of work to be done.

Exploratory pilot project to assess the extent of spouse abuse and family violence in the area based on demographic data gathered during the project. Project research will be used to: 1. document needs of abused spouses. 2. plan and develop services and service-delivery systems. 3. develop community informational packet. The pilot project will begin to coordinate a referral, informational, and educational system for spouse abuse and family violence. We will begin to formulate policies between existing agencies for the treatment and referral of abused spouses. We will generate community support and interest in spouse abuse in order to support and expand services in the future.

OBJECTIVES: Public service to be accomplished, by whom, time frame, and milestones.

1. To refer 10 women per month to the FETC training programs.
2. To introduce 40 women to supportive and informational services.
3. To involve 15 women per month in self-help peer groups.
4. To contact and speak before 12 community groups and agencies per month on spouse abuse and family violence, and the services available through this program.

95

5. To coordinate and formalize policies for treatment of battered and abused women with law enforcement agencies, courts, hospitals, and correctional agencies.

No. of positions				No. of
Part-time	Full-time	Position title	Salary	months
	1	Director	$ 833	9
	2	Counselor/		
		Case manager	750	9
	2	Outreach worker	750	9
	1	Secretary	650	9
5	1	Self Help Facilitator/		
		Liaison	750	9

Employer Job Title	Director
No. Openings	1
Hours	Day and evening
Days	5 days/week
Hrs. per week	40
Starting Salary	$833/month

Duties: Responsible for coordination of entire program.

Responsibilities: Must have knowledge of community resources and good community contacts. Must have knowledge of interviewing skills, crisis intervention, spouse abuse and family violence. Supervisory experience preferred. Ability to coordinate and supervise the budget process. College work preferred. Flexible scheduling necessary.

```
Employer Job Title          Self Help Group Facilitator/
                            Liaison Person
No. Openings                1
Hours                       Day and evening
Days                        5 days/week
Hrs. per week               40
Starting Salary             $750/month
```

Duties: Act as facilitator for many self-help groups
for abused spouses each week. Provide referrals,
supportive services, and advocacy for members of self-
help groups. Participate in community education as
necessary.

Requirements: Experience in the area of spouse abuse
preferred.   Able   to work independently and take
initiative. Responsible, organized and able to keep
accurate records to begin to document the extent of
spouse abuse. Flexible scheduling necessary.

```
Employer Job Title          Counselor/Case manager
No. Openings                2
Hours                       Day and evening
Days                        5 days/week
Hrs. per week               40
Starting Salary             $750/month
```

Duties: Interview abused women who are interested in
the program, develop rapport, and aid clients in the
utilization of services. Do crisis intervention as
necessary. Act as advocate for clients in dealing with
health, welfare, housing and legal services.

Requirements: Good interpersonal skills -- warmth,
empathy, willingness to respect clients' choices, etc.
Previous experience working in a "helping" capacity
preferred.   B.A.   preferred.   Flexible scheduling
necessary.

```
Employer Job Title       Outreach worker/Community
                            Educator
No. Openings             2
Hours                    Day and evening
Days                     5 days/week
Hrs. per week            40
Starting Salary          $750/month
```

Duties: Contact and speak at community agencies, schools, meetings and citizen groups on spouse abuse and family violence.

Requirements: Knowledge of community groups, resources, and agencies. Ability to speak comfortably in front of a wide variety of people. Previous experience in teaching, group leading, and public presentation is preferred. Flexible scheduling is necessary.

```
Employer Job Title       Secretary
No. Openings             1
Hours                    8:00 A.M. - 5:00 P.M.
Days                     5 days/week
Hrs. per week            40
Starting Salary          $650/month
```

Duties: Perform secretarial duties for Director and other staff as needed.

Requirements: Ability to relate to a wide variety of clients that come through the door; warm, relaxed personality. Demonstrated knowledge of grammar, spelling & punctuation. Demonstrated typing skill. Clerical and record-keeping skills. Ability to work on the telephone pleasantly & effectively. Commitment to the area of spouse abuse and family violence.

Administration and Operational Cost Breakdown
-- 9 months --

Supplemental Sheet

A. Rent -- Building
    1000 sq ft @ 35c/sq ft
    $350 per mo x 9 months $3,150.00 $3,150.00

B. Equipment

    1 rebuilt electric typewriter
    $7.00 per mo x 9 months   63.00

    1 dictaphone
    $25per mo x 9 months   135.00

    1 rebuilt desk-top copier
    $20 per mo x 9 months   180.00

    1 projector
    $20 per mo x 9 months   180.00   558.00

C. Utilities & Telephone

    P. G. & E.
    $55 per mo x 9 months   495.00

    Telephone
    5 phones--3 lines--1 hold
    Installation   330.00
    $71.70 per mo service x 9 mo   645.30
    $150 per mo toll &
    long distance x 9 mo   1,350.00   2,820.30

D. Materials/Supplies
    $300 ea for 2 educational films   600.00
    $50 ea for 2 tape recorders   100.00
    $5 per mo for typing & office
    paper x 9 months   45.00
    400 leaflets (8½x14) accordian
    folded, printed leaflets on
    spouse abuse, per mo for
    community education at $30 per
    1000 for 9 months   108.00
    2 staplers at $7.50 ea   15.00
    $15 per mo x 9x 7 employees   945.00   1,813.00

E.   Salaries, Fringe & Travel for
     Administrative Purposes

     Consultation: 2 hrs per mo at
     $20 per hour 18 hrs x $20   360.00

     Travel for Director to visit
     other programs & attend training
     200 miles a mo x 9 x .17
     per mile   306.00   1,581.00

F.   Project Staff Travel

     Outreach Worker for rural areas
     500 miles per mo x 9 x .17   765.00

     Outreach Worker for Fresno area
     300 miles per mo x 9 x .17   459.00   1,224.00

              Total Operational Cost $10,231.80

                SUPPORTIVE SERVICE COST BREAKDOWN

A.   Child Care

     1 child per employee for 1st mo,
     full-time care
     $150 per month x 9 $1,050.00 $1,050.00

Administration & Operational Cost Breakdown

BUDGET LINE ITEMS*	AMOUNTS
a. Rent - Building	$ 3,150.00
b. Equipment Rent_x_ Purchase____	558.00
c. Utilities & Telephone	2,805.00
d. Materials, Supplies	913.00
e. Insurance	-0-
f. Salaries, Fringe, & Travel for Administrative Purposes	1,581.00
g. Project Staff Travel	1,224.00
TOTAL	$ 10,231.00

Supportive Service Cost Breakdown

BUDGET LINE ITEMS*	AMOUNTS
a. Child Care $150 per mo x 7	$ 1,050.00
b. Health & Medical	
c. Assistance in Securing Bonds	
d. Transportation	
e. Clothing, Tools, & Supplies	
TOTAL	$ 1,050.00

*Please provide Formulas used to arrive at Amount

requested for each Line Item in the space below or additional pages as needed.

EXAMPLES: - Utilities $35 mo x 12 mo = $420.00

- Supportive Services (Clothing: $25.00

per participant x 2 participants = $50.00)

101

Federal Employment & Training Commission

CETA Title VI Project Budget

BUDGET LINE ITEMS	AMOUNTS
1. CETA PERSONNEL COSTS	
a. Wages (Participants)	$ 50,472.00
b. Fringe Benefits	5,754.20
2. ADMINISTRATION & OPERATING COSTS	10,231.00
3. SUPPORTIVE SERVICE COSTS	1,050.00
TOTAL CETA COSTS	$ 67,507.00